Cyber Strategy: Risk-Driven Security and Resiliency

Cyber Strategy

Risk-Driven Security and Resiliency

Carol A. Siegel
Mark Sweeney

CRC Press
Taylor & Francis Group
Boca Raton London New York

CRC Press is an imprint of the
Taylor & Francis Group, an **informa** business

AN AUERBACH BOOK

CRC Press
Taylor & Francis Group
6000 Broken Sound Parkway NW, Suite 300
Boca Raton, FL 33487-2742

© 2020 by Taylor & Francis Group, LLC
CRC Press is an imprint of Taylor & Francis Group, an Informa business

No claim to original U.S. Government works

Printed on acid-free paper

International Standard Book Number-13: 978-0-367-33945-6 (Paperback)
978-0-367-45817-1 (Hardback)

Visit the Taylor & Francis Web site at
http://www.taylorandfrancis.com

and the CRC Press Web site at
http://www.crcpress.com

Contents

Author Biographies

 **Carol A. Siegel** is a Cybersecurity strategy and IT Risk Management professional with over 30+ years' experience. Carol earned her BS in Systems Analysis Engineering from Boston University in 1971, and her MBA in Computer Applications from New York University in 1984. She has CISSP, CISA, and CISM certifications from ISC2 and ISACA, respectively. Carol has coauthored one of the first books on Internet security, a book for Microsoft on Windows NT Security, as well as numerous articles for Auerbach Publications on information security and risk management. Carol has worked for many Fortune 50 financial services companies in the Banking, Insurance, Big Four, and Pharma sectors and has held several Chief Information Security Officer (CISO) positions. Most recently, Carol worked for the Federal Reserve Bank of New York.

 **Mark Sweeney** is a Cybersecurity and Cyber Resiliency professional with over 5 years of experience in strategizing and implementing risk-based cybersecurity and cyber resiliency programs. Mark earned his BS in Security & Risk Analysis – Information & Cyber Security from Penn State University in 2014. Mark has worked in Big Four consulting companies and the Financial Services Industry as a Cybersecurity and Cyber Resiliency expert, and he is currently a cyber insurance underwriter.

1 Why Cybersecurity and Cyber Resiliency Strategies Are Mandatory for Organizations Today

Cybersecurity and cyber resiliency are the number one concerns for companies today. Organizations must protect their assets and defend against threats and attacks in order to stay in business. A break-in or breach can destroy a company's assets and/or reputation in a matter of minutes. Readiness is key, so that if the unthinkable happens, your company will have the tools and action plans to counter and recover from the attack.

Developing a cybersecurity and cyber resiliency strategy that supports the business and is resource efficient requires strategic planning. Most organizations lack the necessary experience to conduct the appropriate planning required to streamline efforts, while minimizing risks, as they strive toward their long-term strategic business objectives.

The cybersecurity profession is growing exponentially. Although there are numerous universities and technical schools that provide degrees in these new fields, they are not teaching how to develop a strategy: one that is unifying – that allows an organization to develop a risk-based, efficient, and targeted effort that will be approved by top company management.

The cyber resiliency field is even younger, evolving from the traditional fields of disaster recovery and business continuity. It is, however, not fine-tuned to the cybersecurity threats of today and struggles to identify and prepare for the threats of tomorrow. There is much more growth that must happen in this arena in order for organizations to feel comfortable with their cyber programs in an age of persistent and advancing threats.

In larger organizations, pockets of cybersecurity and cyber resiliency can be found in company silos such as specific business units. A business unit or silo can have its own information security and disaster recovery/business continuity strategy that may or may not roll up into an enterprise-wide effort. Also, if a company has acquired other companies and joined additional networks, each legacy company or business unit will surely have their own policies, procedures, standards, and/or frameworks they follow. All of these strategies may have conflicting goals and not focus on the highest priority business objectives.

In order to respond to today's threats in a cohesive manner, communications and threat intelligence must utilize a common language and risk metrics. Defining a taxonomy for risks, threats, vulnerabilities, and controls will facilitate an effective and measurable response.

1.1   THE VALUE PROPOSITION

This book will provide concepts, processes, roadmaps, project development tools, and reporting templates to be used by any type of company in order to develop their enterprise-wide cybersecurity and cyber resiliency strategies. This book delivers a methodology for companies to bring together their disassociated strategic planning efforts into one corporate-wide strategy that will efficiently utilize resources, target high risk threats, evaluate resultant risk mitigation efforts, while engaging buy-in across the corporate culture, senior management, business silos, and diverse business interests. A mid-level manager, as well as a CISO or CIO, can use this book to create very real strategies that can be published by the Board of the company and approved by their supervisory entities. By using the unifying techniques discussed later, the strategy sponsor can assimilate strategies from other areas of the company that may be in development and align and/or incorporate them into a central enterprise-wide strategy.

The book will discuss the steps and tasks required from conception of the strategy through its planning, creation, success and performance measurement techniques, management reporting, and planning for future ongoing efforts.

1.2   THE 6 STEPs FOR DEVELOPING AND MAINTAINING A CYBERSECURITY AND CYBER RESILIENCY STRATEGY

In order for an organization to develop and maintain its cybersecurity and cyber resiliency strategy, there are 6 major STEPs that should be taken. If performed, the organization's cybersecurity and cyber resiliency strategy will be comprehensive, functional, long lasting, and have continued buy-in and support from senior management. They are:

1. *STEP 1:* Preplanning: Preparation for Strategy Development
2. *STEP 2:* Strategy Project Management
3. *STEP 3:* Cyber Threats, Vulnerabilities, and Intelligence Analysis
4. *STEP 4:* Cyber Risks and Controls
5. *STEP 5:* Current and Target State Assessments
6. *STEP 6:* Strategic Plan Performance Measurement and End of the Year (EoY) Tasks

The 6 Development and Annual Maintenance STEPs for a Cybersecurity and Cyber Resiliency Strategy (Figure 1.1) show a sequential representation of the 6 STEPs required.

Each of the 6 STEPs will be discussed in detail throughout the book and methodologies presented for their approach and execution. *NOTE:* In striving to keep applicability of the strategy particulars and processes presented here current and continuously timely, the authors have decided to make this book technology agnostic, thereby not dating any particular technology, objective, initiative, or conclusion.

FIGURE 1.1　The 6 Development and Annual Maintenance STEPs for a Cybersecurity and Cyber Resiliency Strategy.

1.3　CYBERSECURITY AND CYBER RESILIENCY STRATEGY KEY PLAYERS

What job functions and management levels of people in an organization might need this information? The most obvious people would be any one in the information security, cybersecurity, cyber resiliency, business continuity/disaster recovery, and resiliency areas that are tasked with developing a strategic action plan to combat cyber threats and attacks over the longer term. This would include, but not be limited to, such roles as shown in Table 1.1.

TABLE 1.1

Cybersecurity and Cyber Resiliency Strategy Key Players

Developers, Approvers, or Readers
1. Chief Information Security Officer (CISO)
2. Chief Information Officer (CIO)
3. Chief Technology Officer (CTO)
4. Cyber/Security Architect
5. Cyber/Security Engineer
6. Security Administrator
7. Cyber/Security Manager
8. Security Software Developer
9. Security Incident Responder
10. Cryptographer
11. Cybersecurity/Resiliency Consultant
12. Data Security Strategist
13. Chief Resiliency Officer
14. Business Continuity Analyst
15. Disaster Recovery Manager
16. Resiliency Engineer
17. Business Preparedness and Resiliency Program Manager
18. Global Resiliency Project Manager

However, it is not just the security professionals who need to be concerned with a cyberattack. Increasingly more regulations are demanding accountability from senior management when there is a breach. Not just CISOs and CIOs, but also Chief Operating Officers (COO) and Chief Executive Officers (CEO) can be legally liable. Every level up the food chain can be deemed responsible and might have to pay penalties.

1.4   INITIATING THE STRATEGY

In fact, any one of the above job roles might have already initiated a cybersecurity or cyber resiliency strategy independently. From a top down perspective, it is clearly easier if a strategy is created and approved from a senior manager or c-level position as that level of management can authorize and dedicate the appropriate resources to the task more easily. In addition, a c-level or senior vice president frequently interfaces with governing boards and oversight bodies and is more apt to get buy-in more quickly. However, if the strategy is assigned to a subject matter expert (SME) further down the food chain, this approach will give him/her all the information and steps necessary to work the strategy up the corporate structure and get all the relevant participants involved.

Optimally, a corporate strategy needs to be unified in a top down approach from senior levels, in order to profit from synergies and alignment with business objectives and resources. However, from a bottom up perspective, if a mid-level manager needs to create a strategy, it is strongly advisable that he/she needs to engage and obtain senior management buy-in from the beginning. This can be done via networking, making presentations and awareness sessions, participating in relevant committees, arranging targeted meetings, and setting specific agenda items. Proposing a strategy to senior management should include how the strategy meets overall corporate objectives and aligns with other existing strategies throughout the organization. The list of players that can initiate a strategy can be expanded to literally any group in an organization that needs to develop a long-term strategy, as the objective of this book is to provide the process and approach by which to formulate the strategy and gain its wide-spread adoption.

1.5   TRIGGERS TO CREATE A CORPORATE CYBERSECURITY AND CYBER RESILIENCY STRATEGY

Within any organization there most assuredly exists pressure to create a cybersecurity and cyber resiliency strategy. There is simply too much press for companies not to realize that they need a written strategy, together with procedures in case of an attack or breach. In summary, pressures to create a cybersecurity and cyber resiliency strategy ("the strategy") can include the following triggers as shown in

TABLE 1.2

Cybersecurity and Cyber Resiliency Strategy Triggers

Reactive Triggers	Proactive Triggers
1. Press release	1. Absence of a strategy
2. Cyber threat	2. Unification of strategies
3. System hack or breach	3. Cyber intelligence
4. Assessment report	4. Regulatory requirement
5. Audit finding	5. Business controls
6. Legal issue	

Table 1.2. In the case of a significant security event or an audit finding, the organization will need to move quickly to satisfy this gap.

1.6 INFORMATION SECURITY VS. CYBERSECURITY

In some organizations, cybersecurity is used synonymously with information security, but they are not the same thing. Some basic definitions are in order here.

1.6.1 INFORMATION SECURITY

Information security is defined as the protection of information and information systems from unauthorized access, use, disclosure, disruption, modification, or destruction in order to provide confidentiality, integrity, and availability. According to the International Organization for Standardization (ISO), the model, commonly referred to as "7 ISO principles" is comprised of seven principles: confidentiality, integrity, availability, non-repudiation, accountability, authenticity, and reliability. Confidentiality means that the information should not be made accessible or disclosed to unauthorized individuals, entities, or processes. Integrity is the property of safeguarding the accuracy and completeness of assets. Availability means the property of being accessible and usable upon demand by an authorized entity. Non-repudiation means the ability to prove the occurrence of an action in such a way that the action cannot be repudiated later. Accountability denotes the property which ensures that the identity of the individual, with any type of action, in the information system can be traced. Authenticity refers to entities such as users, processes, systems, and information. Reliability means consistency in the intended behaviors and results.

The three principles most widely referred to – confidentiality, integrity, and availability are known as the CIA Triad. This model is designed to guide policies and standards for information security within organizations. Figure 1.2 shows the CIA Security Triad.

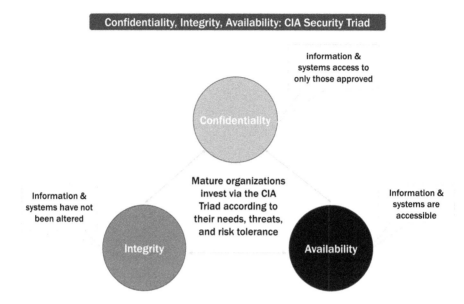

FIGURE 1.2   CIA Security Triad.

1.6.2   CYBERSECURITY

As defined by the National Initiative for Cybersecurity Careers and Studies™ (NICCS), Cybersecurity is strategy, policy, and standards regarding the security of and operations in cyberspace, and encompassing the full range of threat reduction, vulnerability reduction, deterrence, international engagement, incident response, resiliency, and recovery policies and activities, including computer network operations, information assurance, law enforcement, diplomacy, military, and intelligence missions as they relate to the security and stability of the global information and communications infrastructure.

In general, cybersecurity is the ability to protect or defend the cyberspace user from cyberattacks. Based on the definitions, cybersecurity is contained within information security. Figure 1.3 shows the overlapping areas of information security and cybersecurity.

1.7   CYBER RESILIENCY VS. TRADITIONAL RESILIENCY

Cyber resiliency is a new and emerging field that has become front and center with the recent acceptance of the reality that it is no longer if, but when a cyber-attack will occur. Due to this realization, the industry has imported traditional business continuity concepts into the suite of cyber activities and morphed them

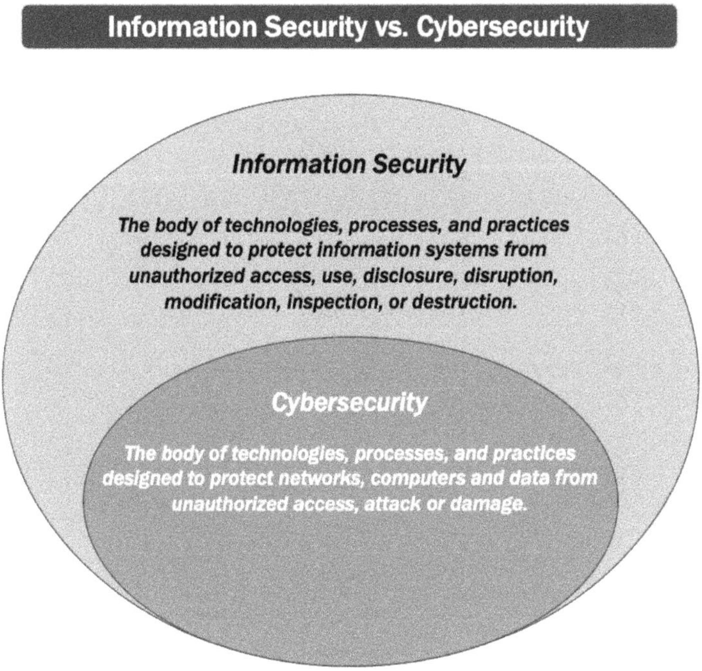

Information Security vs. Cybersecurity

Information Security

The body of technologies, processes, and practices
designed to protect information systems from
unauthorized access, use, disclosure, disruption,
modification, inspection, or destruction.

Cybersecurity

The body of technologies, processes, and practices
designed to protect networks, computers and data from
unauthorized access, attack or damage.

FIGURE 1.3   Information Security vs. Cybersecurity.

to fit the needs of a cyber program. This may not be the best approach in creating a cyber program.

The main goal of a cyber resiliency program within an organization is to develop an array of optimal alternatives for meeting the organization's mission if a cyberattack is to occur – to become resilient from the impacts of a cyberattack. As Figure 1.4 shows, cyber resiliency spreads security, business continuity, and resiliency across a suite of disciplines that organizations must consider in order to be resilient in the face of advancing and persistent cyber threats.

There are many definitions of cyber resiliency depending on the nature of the mission that the organization wants to assure. Below are several definitions.

Cyber resiliency is:

1. The ability of the organization to achieve its mission even under degraded circumstances as defined by the Computer Emergency Response Program (CERT).
2. The organization's ability to adapt to risk that affects its core operational capacities. Operational resiliency is an emergent property of effective operational risk management, supported and enabled by activities such as security and business continuity. A subset of enterprise resiliency, operational resiliency focuses on the organization's ability to manage operational risk,

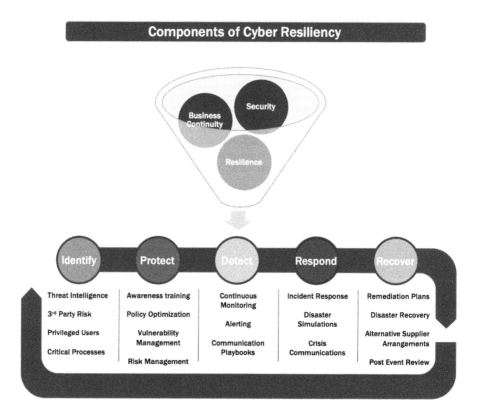

FIGURE 1.4   The Components of Cyber Resiliency.

whereas enterprise resiliency encompasses additional areas of risk such as business risk and credit risk as defined by the CERT.

3. The ability to quickly adapt and recover from any known or unknown changes to the environment through holistic implementation of risk management, contingency, and continuity planning as defined by NIST SP 800-34.

4. The ability to continue to: (i) operate under adverse conditions or stress, even if in a degraded or debilitated state, while maintaining essential operational capabilities; and (ii) recover to an effective operational posture in a time frame consistent with mission needs as defined by NIST SP 800-37.

While some of the definitions vary, the main goal of cyber resiliency is to prepare the organization so that executives, board members, employees, and perhaps even the general public, can be confident that the IT systems supporting the business will complete their designated mission, while under and after an attack.

Figure 1.5 shows the overlapping areas of cybersecurity and cyber resiliency.

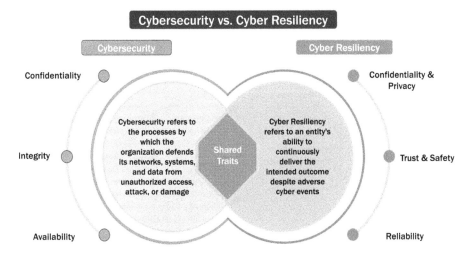

FIGURE 1.5   Cybersecurity vs. Cyber Resiliency.

1.8   CYBERSECURITY AND CYBER RESILIENCY STRATEGY LIFE CYCLE

One of the more differentiating qualities of a cyber strategy from a cyber program is its repeatability or life cycle characteristic. As the 6 STEPs to strategy creation and then subsequent maintenance show, the life cycle starts with assessment, then strategy creation, after that performance management of the strategy and ultimately, the establishment of new initiatives based on the performance of the prior year's initiatives. The process then repeats itself, most likely yearly. Each of the main thrusts of the life cycle have subcomponents that will be expounded upon throughout the following chapters. Figure 1.6 shows a graphical representation of this life cycle.

1.9   CYBER STRATEGIES VS. CYBER PROGRAMS

There can be a lot of confusion on the differences between a cyber strategy and a cyber program. A program is a list of steps that are or will be taken to accomplish specific goals and objectives. A strategy is a list of objectives and fulfillment approaches derived in advance to be achieved at a future time; a future oriented activity that can be represented by a roadmap of actions that it will take to accomplish specific tasks or goals.

A strategy is more comprehensive than a program and is not operational in nature. A strategy has a large scope and may consider multiple approaches in order to achieve the desired target state. A strategy presents the reasons as to why a particular path is taken—the program outlines the how. A strategy is developed before the program and will direct the program.

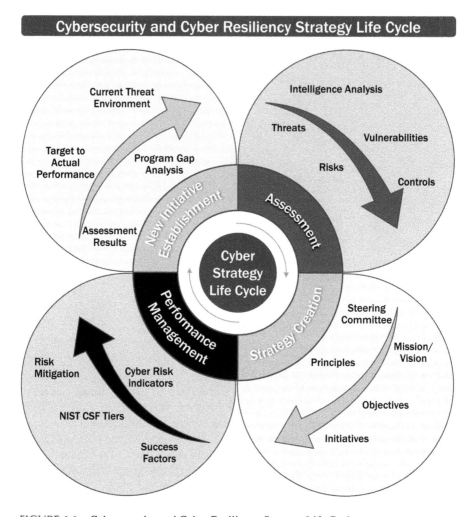

FIGURE 1.6   Cybersecurity and Cyber Resiliency Strategy Life Cycle.

A program is a collection of projects or initiatives and is generally long term and operational in nature. A program can consist of a portfolio of projects that have similar goals or objectives. A program is developed after strategic objectives are formulated. The program is comprised of many projects or initiatives that help achieve those strategic objectives.

Cybersecurity and cyber resiliency strategies begin with overarching missions and/or visions of the organization. The strategy may also require principles. The principles are technology agnostic and may be general in nature. The objectives are derived from the principles and can be one-to-many in nature. Supporting the objectives are the projects or initiatives. Each project or initiative has a project plan or roadmap. A department, functional area, or enterprise can have cyber programs

TABLE 1.3

Attributes of Cyber Strategies and Cyber Programs

Attribute	Cyber Strategy	Cyber Program
1. Strategic in Nature	✓	
2. Operational in Nature		✓
3. Multi-Year	✓	✓
4. Repetitive Life Cycle	✓	
5. Contains Mission and/or Vision	✓	
6. Contains Principles	✓	
7. Contains Objectives	✓	✓
8. References Projects/Initiatives	✓	✓
9. Implements Projects/Initiatives		✓

that encompass one or more cyber strategies and/or cyber programs. The objective of this book is to help organizations to incorporate top-down approaches to developing their cyber strategies. Different cyber programs can then be developed according to organizational structure and objectives. Table 1.3 highlights the major differences between the two.

1.10 CYBERSECURITY AND CYBER RESILIENCY PROGRAMS FOR ORGANIZATIONS

However, cybersecurity and cyber resiliency programs can consist of many of the same elements as shown in Figure 1.7.

A cybersecurity/cyber resiliency program is ongoing and always operational within the organization. It is built over time and refined as needed depending on security threats/risks and business needs. A program includes defined initiatives, procedures, and controls. It defines not only technical but managerial, operational, legal, and regulatory measures. It is built to address the organizational pillars of people, process, and technology. The program is constructed utilizing security architecture principles, so that there can exist technical uniformity and resiliency from a ground up perspective incorporating controls at the data, operating system, application, network, Internet, and cloud levels. These controls maintain the systems quality attributes of classic CIA plus accountability and assurance. Both the cybersecurity strategy and program(s) are based on a corporate vision and principles. Where the cybersecurity program differs from the cybersecurity strategy is that the program is ongoing, and providing for and creating the actual technical security infrastructure for the organization, while the cybersecurity strategy, based on intelligence and risk-based threat analysis, proposes strategic objectives that can vary over time. In order to satisfy these strategic objectives, specific initiatives must be crafted and implemented. These initiatives over time may influence the cybersecurity posture and underlying enterprise security architecture, resulting in changes in technology and processes.

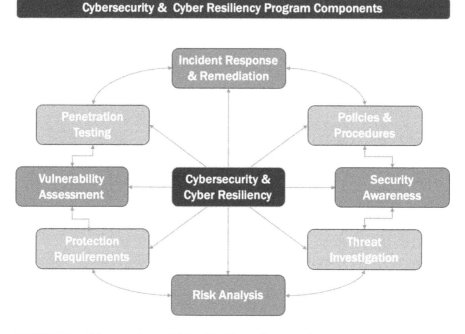

FIGURE 1.7   Cybersecurity and Cyber Resiliency Program Components.

1.11   CYBERSECURITY AND CYBER RESILIENCY ARCHITECTURE: STANDARDS AND FRAMEWORKS

A documented enterprise-wide security architecture is critical in establishing the foundation for any cyber program. The security architecture generally would be developed by the Information Technology (IT), Architecture, and/or Engineering groups. Having an enterprise security architecture has many critical business and technical benefits, some of which are listed in Table 1.4.

TABLE 1.4

Benefits of an Enterprise Cyber Architecture

Business Benefits	Technical Benefits
• Alignment with enterprise objectives	• Provide resilient services
• Remain current with changing requirements	• Security and Resiliency by design
• Minimize risk through technical choices	• Network segmentation to provide containment
• Detect and react to threats more quickly	• Provide isolation and redundancy
• Separation of duties	• Ensure availability
	• Address threats with technology choices
	• Defense in Depth

Without a cybersecurity or cyber resilient architecture, the applicable tools and techniques would not be able to be deployed to prevent or recover from a cyberattack.

1.11.1 ENTERPRISE INFORMATION SECURITY ARCHITECTURE

Security procedures and products are, of course, critical to maintaining a security and resilient infrastructure, but more foundational to the choice of products are the industry standards and frameworks that the organization chooses to follow. Figure 1.8 shows a classic organization security architecture and how data and critical assets and the missions and business processes they support are key to cybersecurity and cyber resiliency. The diagram also shows how a Defense in Depth approach is key to implementing, maintaining, monitoring, and measuring cybersecurity and cyber resiliency. Additionally, groups such as Audit, Legal, and Compliance play an important role in assisting the implementation of cyber program, the cyber strategies and their goals. Cyber programs and strategies are not just about implementation and maintenance, but also about monitoring and reporting on all aspects to executives as to their effectiveness and relevance.

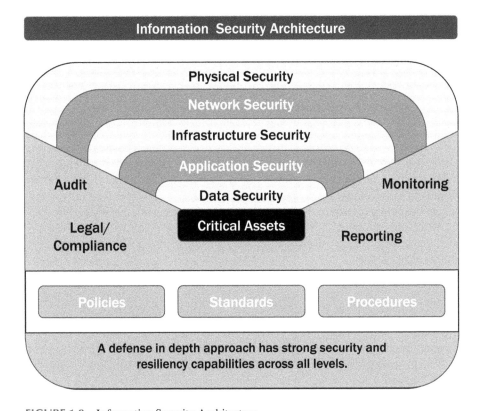

FIGURE 1.8   Information Security Architecture.

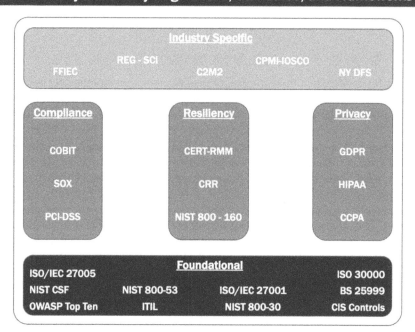

FIGURE 1.9   Regulatory Cybersecurity Architecture.

1.11.2 REGULATORY SECURITY ARCHITECTURE

In order to provide more structure to the strategy, appropriate standards and frameworks need to be selected and endorsed by the organization. There exist a number of industry standards and frameworks that can be utilized as a basis for the strategy, and/or can be used for assessing the strategy current and target states. Some of the most recognized and accepted are listed in Figure 1.9.

Implementing the required business sector regulations is fundamental in preventing fraud and deception. A solid regulatory architecture will provide the basis for the organization to meet business objectives, provide system reliability, and protect against legal liability.

1.11.3 INTRODUCTION TO THE NIST CYBERSECURITY FRAMEWORK (CSF)

A corporate cyber strategy and/or program can have many components. There are many industry standards, frameworks, and guidelines that can inform a cyber resiliency strategy. One of the most commonly known cybersecurity frameworks that also encompasses cyber resiliency aspects is the NIST Cybersecurity Framework (CSF). The CSF consists of three main components: The Core, Implementation Tiers, and Profiles. As shown in Figure 1.10 the CSF Core

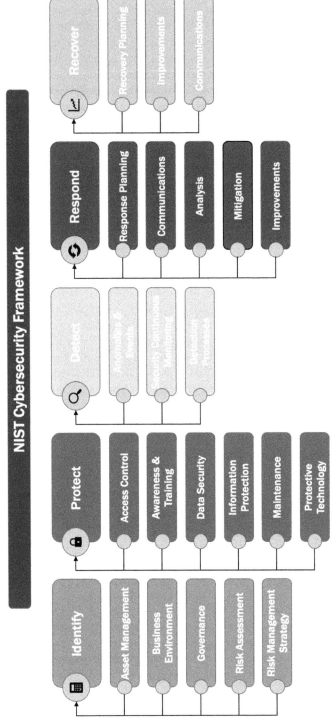

FIGURE 1.10   The NIST Cybersecurity Framework (CSF).

provides a set of five desired cybersecurity functions: Identify, Protect, Detect, Respond, and Recover. This core was designed in order to help organizations manage and reduce their cybersecurity and cyber resiliency risks in an easily digestible way. Taking a more detailed approach, the five functions are then split into 23 categories of cybersecurity activities. The 23 categories are then broken down into 108 sub-categories, but more on this in later chapters. A good cyber resiliency program, guided by the cyber resiliency strategy, should be spread across all areas of the CSF Framework Core, but may not necessarily cover all 23 categories of cybersecurity activities.

By choosing the NIST CSF as the framework with which to align their resiliency activities, the most mature organizations will utilize the NIST CSF in ways that are most relevant for their business needs and associated risks. This is called a Framework Profile. Profiles will be unique to organizations and are a balance of requirements, objectives, risk appetite, and resources against the desired outcomes of the Framework Core. Later chapters will also outline how Profiles can be used to identify opportunities for improvement by comparing a Current Profile with a Target Profile.

1.12   CYBER PROGRAM PREPLANNING

Before an organization can start to develop a cybersecurity or a cyber resiliency strategy, there is a significant amount of top-level corporate planning that needs to occur and be ongoing. For the safety of the organization, a cyber program that addresses both cybersecurity and cyber resiliency should be in development or already implemented. Some of the major areas that need preplanning in order to support an enterprise-wide cyber program are shown in Figure 1.11.

These areas together with extensive project planning techniques and templates will be addressed in Chapters 2 and 3.

1.13   TECHNICAL AREAS OF CONCENTRATION
FOR A CYBER PROGRAM

In order to achieve the level of security desired by the organization, the infrastructure will need to be continuously updated and monitored. There are some fundamental technological areas that all organizations must have that are operational with dedicated initiatives and programs in place to develop, operate, and monitor them. Please note this list is not exhaustive or completely necessary for every program. It is up to the organization to decide what aspects of a cyber program is necessary and which is the most important. However, Table 1.5 is a good place to start when building a cyber program to ensure that the standard bases are covered.

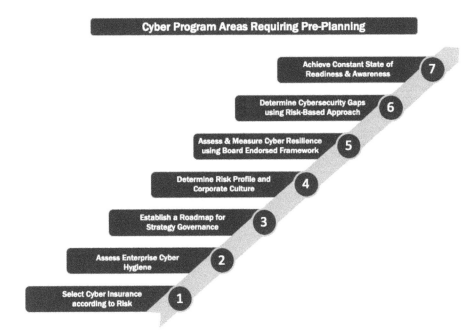

FIGURE 1.11   Cyber Program Areas Requiring Preplanning.

TABLE 1.5

Typical Domains of a Cyber Program

1. Systems Administration
2. Security Architecture and Engineering
3. Identity and Access Management
4. Network Security
5. Application Security
6. Data Protection and Cryptography
7. Endpoint Security
8. Infrastructure Security
9. Logging and Monitoring
10. Vulnerability and Patch Management
11. Availability, Redundancy, and Resiliency
12. Incident Response
13. Asset Management and Inventory
14. Security Operations
15. Third Party & Supply Chain Management
16. Audit
17. Legal
18. Compliance

FIGURE 1.12   The 6 Development and Annual Maintenance STEPs for a Cybersecurity and Cyber Resiliency Strategy.

All of these areas are standard components in a comprehensive Cyber Program and should be ongoing areas of concentration for all organizations.

Following the 6 STEPs as shown in Figure 1.12, Chapter 2 will present Preplanning: Preparation for Strategy Development (STEP 1).

2 The 6 STEPs in Developing and Maintaining a Cybersecurity and Cyber Resiliency Strategy

There are 6 major STEPs that should be taken in order for an organization to develop and maintain its cybersecurity and cyber resiliency strategy. Figure 2.1 shows a graphical representation of the 6 STEPs required to develop and maintain a cybersecurity and cyber resiliency strategy. This chapter provides an overview of what is contained in each of the STEPs, and then subsequent chapters discuss each STEP in more detail.

2.1 STEP 1: PREPLANNING: PREPARATION FOR STRATEGY DEVELOPMENT

Preparation is key in order to create a receptive environment for strategy creation and ultimate acceptance. There are a number of topics that need to be considered before starting to write the strategy. Understanding the corporate culture is the first step toward strategy development.

2.1.1 CORPORATE CULTURE AND ORGANIZATIONAL ANALYSIS

The approach to developing the strategy depends greatly on the culture of the organization. The beliefs, ideologies, values, and principles of an organization form

The 6 Development and Annual Maintenance STEPs for a Cybersecurity and Cyber Resiliency Strategy

FIGURE 2.1   The 6 Development and Maintenance Steps for a Cybersecurity and Cyber Resiliency Strategy.

its culture. Organizational culture is a system of shared assumptions, values, and beliefs, which governs how people behave in organizations. These shared values have a strong influence on the people in the organization and dictate how they communicate with others and perform their jobs.

According to Robert E. Quinn and Kim S. Cameron at the University of Michigan at Ann Arbor, from their article "Competing Values Framework", there are four types of organizational culture: Clan, Adhocracy, Market, and Hierarchy as shown in Figure 2.2.

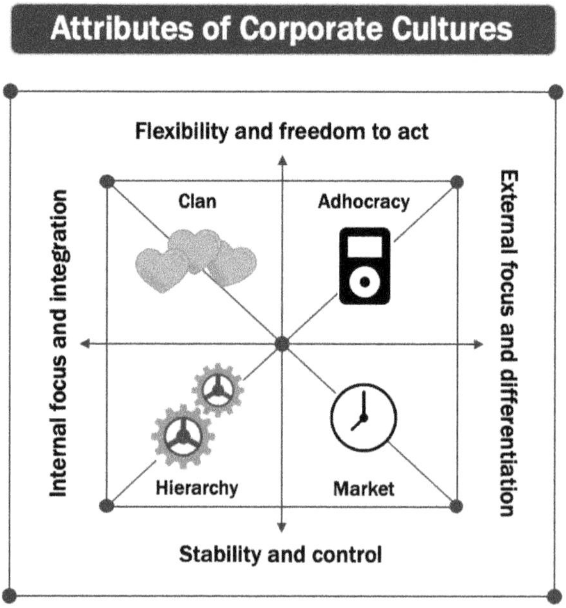

Attributes of Corporate Cultures

Flexibility and freedom to act

Internal focus and integration

Clan   Adhocracy

External focus and differentiation

Hierarchy   Market

Stability and control

FIGURE 2.2   Attributes of Corporate Cultures.

Clan-oriented cultures are family-like, with a focus on mentoring, nurturing, and doing things together. Teamwork, collaboration, and consensus of opinion are paramount. This type of corporate culture may require the most influencing effort to get everyone on board with a unified, corporate-wide strategy. The decision-making process may take longer as all parties need to be in agreement.

Adhocracy-oriented cultures are dynamic and entrepreneurial. They value risk-taking, innovation, adaptability, growth, and produce cutting edge services or products. These kinds of cultures will definitely have an effect on the level of risk appetite and tolerance that will be established for the organization. Strategic objectives will be more aggressive in this case and projects more creative.

Market-oriented cultures are results oriented and focus on getting the job done. They value competition, achievement, and are customer driven. Their goal is to provide services for their customers. These types of organizations may be more risk tolerant.

Hierarchy-oriented cultures are ordered, structured, and controlled, with a focus on efficiency, stability, and coordination. Lead by an administrator, they are bonded by rules, and adhere to identified best practices.

Knowing and understanding the culture of the organization will set the stage for identifying the key players, locating the existing cybersecurity and cyber resiliency efforts under way and understanding the degree and nature of influencing that may be required. There may be various pockets of cybersecurity and cyber resiliency efforts happening throughout the organization without coordination. There also may be one or more centralized cyber programs. Whether there are one or many, a corporate/enterprise level cyber strategy must be created to unify the programs and set the overall corporate direction efficiently, accurately, and based on the corporate risk policies.

2.1.2 Matrixed Organizational Structure

Some types of organizations are highly matrixed, where strategy development can occur in multiple areas as shown in Figure 2.3. In this organization, for example, cyber strategies might be initiated by a project manager in the Investment Trading department. Another strategy might be authorized for development in the Consumer Credit division and yet another under Insurance Products, while another division, Regional Banking, may not have a strategy at all. Checks in the diagram below indicate that a strategy was or is being currently written.

The potential end result of a matrixed organizational structure that publishes multiple cyber strategies is:

- An inefficient use of resources
- Duplicate/redundant initiatives
- A strategy that may not be useful for other areas of the organization; in fact, it may well be in contrast

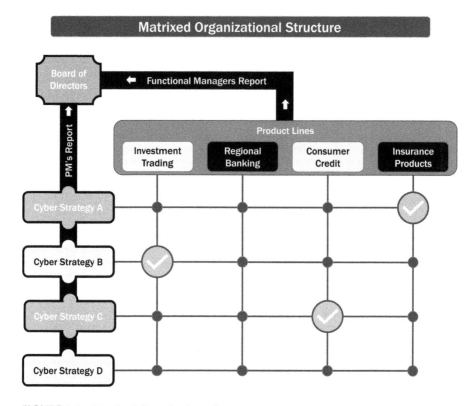

FIGURE 2.3   Matrixed Organizational Structure.

- A strategy that was not sanctioned by a cross-functional team such as a Steering Committee and therefore won't gain top management support or get governance approval
- A strategy that does not align with the vision, principles, and risk policies of the organization

2.1.3 SILOED ORGANIZATIONAL STRUCTURE

Another complexity can occur if an organization has many silos. Silos can be stand-alone departments, acquired companies or merged entities that all report into the same corporate management. In these cases, decisions are made within the silo alone to develop a strategy that pertains just to the silo itself. No collaboration will occur across silos as there is an imaginary wall separating them. The strategies might only come to be reviewed at the board level when they are completely formed. Hence, no synergies or commonality of efforts are achieved. Figure 2.4 shows an example of how communication can go up and down a silo, but not across silos. This is a very common structure for many organizations.

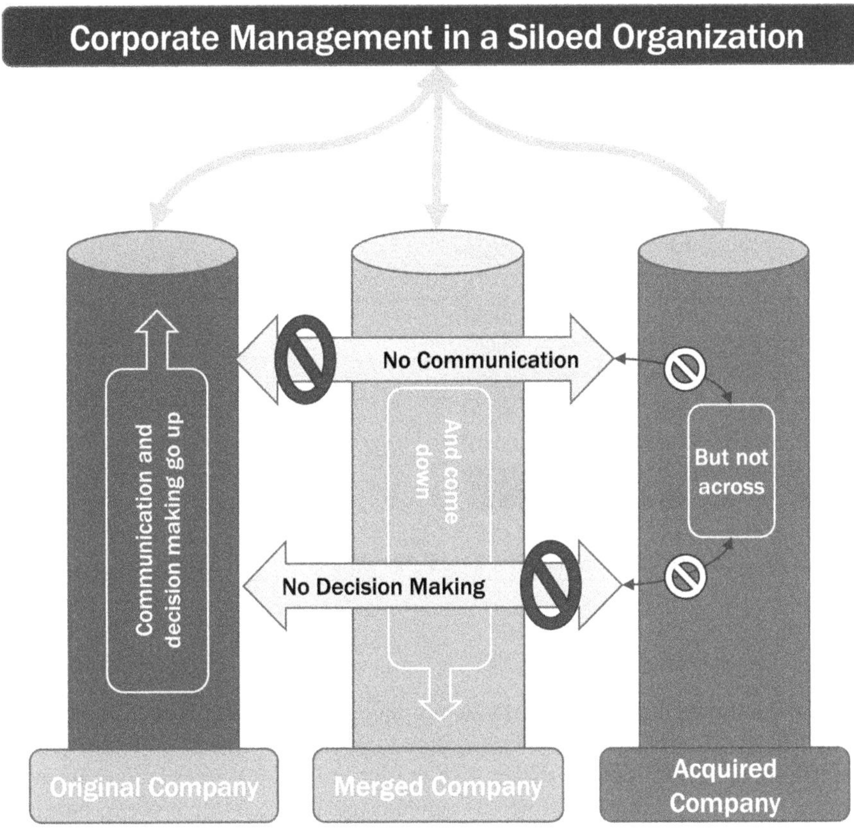

Corporate Management in a Siloed Organization

No Communication

Communication and decision making go up

And come down

But not across

No Decision Making

Original Company

Merged Company

Acquired Company

FIGURE 2.4   Siloed Organizational Structure.

2.1.4   ENABLING THE ORGANIZATION FOR STRATEGY ADOPTION

Whatever kind of organization exists, there are some critical initial steps that must be taken by senior management in order to prepare for the creation of an enterprise-level strategy:

1. Assemble a Strategy Steering Committee
2. Identify the technology risk and control areas to be involved
3. Select the SMEs that will be writing the actual strategy

Each of these points are critical in ensuring that the ultimate strategy will be representative, accurate, risk-based, and adopted. The more complete list of preparatory steps is shown in Figure 2.5.

Steps for Organizational Readiness for a Cyber Strategy

Include Cybersecurity and Cyber Resiliency in the Corporate Awareness Program

Ensure ownership at the C-Suite

Create the appropriate cyber risk steering committee

Inventory existing and planned cyber strategies

Adopt the corporate risk tolerance/risk appetite

Determine the high-level business risks

Obtain threat intelligence sources

Necessary for Strategy Development

FIGURE 2.5   Organizational Readiness for a Cyber Strategy.

2.1.5 Forming a Steering Committee

Once the corporate culture has been determined, the next step is to identify key stakeholders and form a Steering Committee to oversee the plan development and establish the life cycle. Identifying key stakeholders is one of the most important pre-planning activities. Stakeholders can be active or not active in the process, but still have influence over the outcome. Depending on the type of corporate culture, the Steering Committee may be comprised of different types of members. Ideally, there should be a significant number of some of the top-ranking members of the organization, so that decisions can more easily be made and adhered to.

The proper creation of the Steering Committee will significantly help in the elimination of creation and future adoption problems. Critical for inclusion in the Steering Committee are the following corporate roles—VP or greater is preferred (VPs can delegate accordingly for meeting attendance) as shown in Table 2.1.

TABLE 2.1
Steering Committee Members

• Chief Information Security Officer(s) (CISO)	• Production Environments
• Chief Technology Officer(s) (CTO)	• Program Management
• Chief Risk Officer(s) (CRO)	• Audit
• Disaster Recovery/Business Continuity	• Legal
• Business Resiliency	• Compliance
• IT Infrastructure	• Subject Matter Experts (SME)
• IT Architecture	

TABLE 2.2

Critical Success Factors

- Reduced residual risk
- Completed by due date
- Meets stated objectives or requirements
- Compliant with relevant regulations, standards, and policies
- Reduced resource opportunity cost
- Aligns with approved cyber strategies

- Maintains budgetary constraints
- Supported by senior management
- Efficient use of resources
- Approved by all parties
- Maps to corporate goals

Also mandatory for inclusion are the subject matter experts (SME) for cybersecurity and cyber resiliency. The SMEs will determine the criticality, viability, and accuracy of the resultant strategic objectives, initiatives/projects, and timelines.

2.1.6 CREATING STRATEGIC PLAN CRITICAL SUCCESS FACTORS

Critical success factors for any plan can be based on many aspects of an operational environment. Some classic success factors can be economic, regulatory, technical, and cultural in nature. Table 2.2 lists some common success factors used for initiatives. Zoning in on the ones that are relevant to the strategic objectives is an exercise that needs to be addressed by the Steering Committee or sub-committee thereof in order to document the current state. They can be revisited during the final Strategy Plan Performance evaluation phase. Key Performance Indicators (KPIs) and Key Risk Indicators (KRIs) can also be used to measure the success of the strategy, and the degree of risk mitigation. These three measures of plan performance will be reviewed in Chapter 7: Measuring Strategic Plan Performance and End of Year (EoY) Tasks.

2.1.7 DESIGNATING A PROJECT MANAGER FOR THE STEERING COMMITTEE

Once the Steering Committee is formed, it is advisable to identify a project manager (PM), someone who is responsible for scheduling meetings, setting up dial-in numbers, video calls, taking notes, issuing meeting minutes, and following up on action items. The PM can be appointed by the Project Management Office (PMO) and ideally would have a Project Management Professional (PMP) certification. In this manner, the PM could also create a timeline with milestones for the project as well as an action item log and risk register. Budgeting and resource information can also be tracked, with interim reports to designated parties as to the progress of the Steering Committee and the strategic plan development.

2.1.8 DEVELOPING STEERING COMMITTEE TASKS

The Steering Committee will establish all the administrative requirements of the committee and set the overall timeline for the work of the Committee. The tasks will cover the strategy preparation, development, progress reporting, getting governance approvals, and ongoing maintenance. The individual tasks will be itemized in detail

TABLE 2.3

Typical Corporate Business Values

Financial Benefits	Nonfinancial Benefits
• Risk Reduction/Mitigation	• Company Image
• Productivity	• Stewardship
• Efficiency	• Judgment
• Simplicity	• Diversity
• Quality of Service	• Human Capital
• Collaboration	
• Increased Confidentiality, Integrity, and Availability (CIA)	
• Innovation	
• Reliability	
• Cost Avoidance	
• Consistency	

in the Responsible, Accountable, Consulted, Informed (RACI) diagram, for each of the corresponding responsible entities. Undoubtedly, there will be organizational pressures to finish the strategy development, but preparation and organization will ensure a quality product and one that will endure for the desired timeframe. The Steering Committee will loop in other key individuals and/or projects that can help develop and maintain the final strategy deliverable.

2.1.9 ESTABLISHING CORPORATE BUSINESS VALUES

Establishing corporate business values is important for all organizations. It sets the goals and tone of the organization. Corporate programs and efforts must center around those values chosen and further their progression. Table 2.3 shows some of the corporate business values commonly used. Note that companies may see some of the values listed below as financial benefits that are listed as nonfinancial benefits or vice versa. These business values most likely have already been established at a high level in the organization and might be documented in an existing paper or presentation. It is preferable to be in sync with the established, published corporate values. Note that these may change from year to year.

2.1.10 DETERMINING THE MISSION/VISION, PRINCIPLES, AND STRATEGIC OBJECTIVES FOR CYBERSECURITY AND CYBER RESILIENCY

The creation of any cyber strategy must start with a mission or vision. This mission should be enterprise-wide and incorporate some of the already established visions and goals of the organization. The mission or vision should be founded on principles. The principles also should be enterprise-wide and ideally be derived from a published framework or regulation. The framework can be an internally developed one, or one published by a standards body or industry association.

Mission/Vision, Principles, Strategic Objectives, and Initiatives Pyramid

FIGURE 2.6   Mission/Vision, Principles, Strategic Objectives, and Initiatives Pyramid.

Supporting those principles are the strategic objectives. Implementing the objectives will be specific initiatives or projects. The relationship of the mission/vision to principles is a one to many. Similarly, the relationship of the objectives to principles and the initiatives to strategic objectives are also one to many. The Pyramid in Figure 2.6 shows the cascading, one to many relationships between the Mission/Vision, Principles, Strategic Objectives, and Initiatives.

2.1.10.1   Mission/Vision

The first task for the Steering Committee to agree on is the overall mission and vision of the cybersecurity and cyber resiliency strategy. This will set the stage and the tone for the direction of the strategy and the objectives that follow. The mission and vision must reflect the organization as a whole and be in harmony with the organization's overall goals and business objectives. Examples of cyber strategy mission and vision statements are shown in Table 2.4.

TABLE 2.4

Examples of Cyber Strategy Mission/Vision Statements

1. Achieve the best in breed cybersecurity and cyber resiliency programs
2. Protect the organization's assets from cyberattacks
3. Mitigate cyber risk to desired levels in accordance with the company risk tolerance standards
4. Provide exceptional cybersecurity and cyber resiliency services to our clients and business partners
5. Align cybersecurity and cyber resiliency strategies across the enterprise

TABLE 2.5
Examples of Cyber Strategy Principles

1. The CIA principle (Confidentiality, Integrity, and Availability): three key principles which should be strived for in all secure systems
2. The Principle of Least Privilege: any user, program, or process should have only the bare minimum privileges necessary to perform its function
3. Cybersecurity and cyber resiliency programs must be able to adapt rapidly to emerging threats, new technologies, and business models
4. The Principle of Defense in Depth: multilayered security mechanisms with intentional redundancies which increase the system security as a whole
5. Create Value: resources expended to mitigate risk should be less than the consequence of inaction

2.1.10.2   Cyber Program Principles

The second task for the Steering Committee is to agree on the principles of the cybersecurity and cyber resiliency strategy. This will define further the direction of the strategy and the objectives that follow. The mission and vision must reflect the organization as a whole and be in harmony with the organization's overall goals and business objectives. Examples of potential cyber program principles are shown in Table 2.5.

2.1.10.3   Strategic Objectives

Strategic objectives are long-term organizational goals that contribute to achieving the organization's mission or vision. The objective should state a business need that can be quantified and measured. The measurement can be in percentage increase, dollars saved, and/or risk reduced via key risk indicators (KRIs) which will be discussed in Chapter 5. The objective can also indicate a timeframe for success or rate of increase/decrease. Objectives can be general or more granular in nature. For each of the objectives, there will be a series of initiatives or projects that will collectively strive to achieve the objective. Tables 2.6 and 2.7 show examples of cybersecurity and cyber resiliency strategic objectives, respectively.

TABLE 2.6
Examples of Cybersecurity Strategic Objectives

1. Develop a cybersecurity implementation plan
2. Integrate "security by design" into the System Development Life Cycle (SDLC) process
3. Determine future initiatives based on risk, threats, gaps, and performance
4. Increase cybersecurity awareness
5. Implement a risk-based asset protection program

TABLE 2.7

Examples of Cyber Resiliency Strategic Objectives

1. Create a cyber resiliency implementation plan
2. Build a resilient, compartmentalized technical architecture to expedite redundancy and segmentation, promoting accelerated recovery from a cyberattack
3. Develop an X-hour recovery plan from a cyberattack
4. Develop plans and procedures to support the business in a compromised state
5. Implement a risk-based incident response plan for critical business units and systems

2.2   STEP 2: STRATEGY PROJECT MANAGEMENT

For each of the strategic objectives, there will need to be an implementation plan. This is a tactical plan that may contain many individual projects over varying time-frames. Each project and/or initiative, however, will relate back to a specific strategic objective.

2.2.1   INITIATIVES FOR CYBERSECURITY STRATEGIC OBJECTIVES

Tables 2.8 through 2.12 present examples of initiatives for each of the five Cybersecurity Strategic Objectives listed in Table 2.6. Listed are some examples of initiatives that might roll up into that specific strategic objective.

TABLE 2.8

Examples of Initiatives for the 1st Cybersecurity Strategic Objective

Cybersecurity Objective #1: "Develop a Cybersecurity Implementation Plan"
Corresponding Initiatives:

1. Perform a risk assessment(s) to quantify the current state
2. Perform a gap analysis between current and target states to determine potential areas of additional resource investment
3. Map the alignment with the current cybersecurity strategies and programs with business needs and corporate goals
4. Document all cyber business risks within a risk register and indicate compensating controls
5. Conduct a cost-benefit analysis of hiring a consultancy vs. using in-house talent to develop the strategic implementation plan

TABLE 2.9

Examples of Initiatives for the 2nd Cybersecurity Strategic Objective

Cybersecurity Objective #2: "Integrate "Security by Design" into the SDLC Process"
Corresponding Initiatives:

1. Adopt a formal Software Development Life Cycle (SDLC) process for software design
2. Ensure that security requirements are defined and documented in the business requirements gathering and analysis phase
3. Perform threat modeling techniques on systems and applications to determine weak points
4. Deploy the principles of least privilege, defense in depth, and separation of duties when creating and maintaining secure SDLC environments
5. Execute and document quality assurance protocols at every phase of the SDLC

TABLE 2.10

Examples of Initiatives for the 3rd Cybersecurity Strategic Objective

Cybersecurity Objective #3: "Determine Future Initiatives Based on Risk, Threats, Gaps, and Performance"
Corresponding Initiatives:

1. Select or develop a company-wide risk analysis methodology to analyze and prioritize cyber threats
2. Using this risk-based approach, evaluate the current state risk of each asset and determine the target state risk of each asset
3. Perform the gap analysis and compare the actual year end performance to the desired target state
4. Analyze the concentration of the initiatives within each of the Cyber Security Framework (CSF) capabilities and evaluate their risk mitigation performance
5. Based on risk mitigation estimates, target state gaps, current threats and vulnerabilities, determine the areas of future initiative concentration

TABLE 2.11

Examples of Initiatives for the 4th Cybersecurity Strategic Objective

Cybersecurity Objective #4: "Increase Cybersecurity Awareness"
Corresponding Initiatives:

1. Develop a Cybersecurity Awareness Program
2. Advertise elements of the awareness program on the premises of the organization and online as well
3. Implement phishing or other tests to determine the level of compliance with the Awareness Program
4. For those who repeatedly fail the tests, implement training courses to improve compliance, and possibly a temporary reduction of system privileges
5. Advertise group results of the tests to promote compliance

TABLE 2.12

Examples of Initiatives for the 5th Cybersecurity Strategic Objective

Cybersecurity Objective #5: "Implement a Risk-Based Asset Protection Program"
Corresponding Initiatives:

1. Develop and implement a comprehensive asset protection program consisting of asset, vulnerability, patching, logging, monitoring, and alerting management modules for the complete inventory of all technology assets
2. Utilizing the approved company-wide risk analysis methodology, calculate the risk associated with each asset, and develop specific protection protocols per asset
3. Create a cyber threat intelligence program that collects and analyzes current threat information regarding cyberattacks in order to contribute to the overall asset risk calculation
4. Develop a methodology of mapping assets (people, processes, technology) to initiatives in order to determine the total risk scores of each initiative
5. Develop a standard cyber hygiene approach by implementing critical security controls

Note: Some of the initiatives mentioned within the Cybersecurity and Cyber Resiliency Strategic Objectives refer to methodologies and calculations contained within subsequent sections of this book. They will become evident as the reader progresses through the book.

2.2.2 INITIATIVES FOR CYBER RESILIENCY STRATEGIC OBJECTIVES

Tables 2.13 through 2.17 present examples of initiatives for the Cyber Resiliency Strategic Objectives shown in Table 2.7. Following is a list of initiatives examples that might roll up into that specific strategic objective.

The tables above show examples of potential initiatives. In some cases, these are high-level initiatives – in others, they are more granular. They are meant to be representative of the kinds of projects that could be launched, and to provoke thought.

TABLE 2.13

Examples of Initiatives for the 1st Cyber Resiliency Strategic Objective

Cyber Resiliency Objective #1: "Create a Cyber Resiliency Implementation Plan"
Corresponding Initiatives:

1. Determine the recovery requirements for the critical business units of the organization
2. Inventory all Resiliency, Disaster Recovery, and Business Continuity plans and procedures across the enterprise
3. Document the current state network architecture for critical business units and their dependencies
4. Select an appropriate cyber insurance policy
5. Align all resiliency efforts across the enterprise to gain senior management support and efficiencies of scale

TABLE 2.14
Examples of Initiatives for the 2nd Cyber Resiliency Strategic Objective

Cyber Resiliency Objective #2: "Build a Resilient, Compartmentalized Technical Architecture to Facilitate Redundancy and Segmentation"
Corresponding Initiatives:

1. Design a target state technical architecture including Data, Applications, Network, and the Cloud
2. Perform various risk assessments across the current state technical architecture
3. Inventory all resiliency and business continuity technological capabilities across the enterprise in order to gage current cyberattack response potential
4. Segment the technical architecture according to risk level
5. Document and isolate any end-of-life or out of support systems and/or applications

TABLE 2.15
Examples of Initiatives for the 3rd Cyber Resiliency Strategic Objective

Cyber Resiliency Objective #3: "Develop an X-Hour Recovery Plan from a Cyberattack"
Corresponding Initiatives:

1. Evaluate supply chain chokepoints for IT services and understand critical third party services
2. Perform Cyber War Gaming exercises to understand resilience and recovery of IT, processes, and businesses
3. Create a plan for dual site failover and recovery
4. Develop a list of critical systems, applications, and businesses in priority order
5. Document and test against established Recovery Time Objectives (RTO) and Recovery Point Objectives (RPO)

TABLE 2.16
Examples of Initiatives for the 4th Cyber Resiliency Strategic Objective

Cyber Resiliency Objective #4: "Develop Plans and Procedures to Support the Business in a Compromised State"
Corresponding Initiatives:

1. Review any contracts with in-house providers or outside vendors regarding the provision of services in a breach situation
2. Physically document cyber insurance policies and contact information
3. Determine if manual processes can fulfill business needs during periods of IT unavailability
4. Schedule biannual attack and penetration tests to practice all incident response plans
5. Participate and collaborate in industry-wide cyber resiliency industry and gaming events

TABLE 2.17

Examples of Initiatives for the 5th Cyber Resiliency Strategic Objective

Cyber Resiliency Objective #5: "Implement a Risk-Based Incident Response Plan for Critical Business Units or Systems"

Corresponding Initiatives:

1. Perform a threat analysis for critical systems and high-risk areas
2. Create or update incident response plans based on calculated risk levels and current threats
3. Implement a 24/7 Incident Response Team inclusive of digital forensics
4. Issue a Request for Information (RFI) and select a breach response vendor
5. Develop a failover capability using alternate technologies to carry out business processes

2.2.3 CREATING A STRATEGY PROJECT CHARTER

A project to create an enterprise cybersecurity and cyber resiliency strategic plan will likely require an official project charter. Here is where the representative from the Project Management Office can work closely with the other Steering Committee members to decide on some required entries needed to complete the project charter and gain official acceptance into the PMO database and process. The entries into the project charter may be weighted and ranked along with other projects. This weighting may ultimately determine priorities, resource allocations, and budget assignments. Mandatory fields in a basic project charter might be like the following Table 2.18.

A graphic layout for this project charter will be presented in STEP 2: Strategy Project Management that can be downloaded as well from the CRC Press website.

2.2.4 ALIGNING THE STRATEGY WITH OTHER EXISTING CORPORATE STRATEGIES AND CORPORATE BUSINESS OBJECTIVES

One of the first tasks for the Steering Committee is to perform a corporate wide inventory to discover all existing cyber strategies and those being planned and/ or mandated for the future. It is imperative that the resultant cybersecurity and

TABLE 2.18

Sample Basic Project Charter Fields

- Project Manager, Sponsor
- Project Start & Finish Dates
- Business Need
- Scope and Deliverables
- Risks & Issues
- Budget
- Gantt Chart
- Steering Committee Members
- Governance Board(s) Approval

cyber resiliency strategy being developed by this group either supersedes the existing strategies, incorporates them, or is in alignment with them. If not, the strategies produced by this Steering Committee may not ultimately achieve success and acceptance. Once the inventory is complete, it may be advisable for the Steering Committee to invite the sponsor(s) and/or authors of the other strategies to a meeting to discuss differences and potential alignments. At this time, a draft alignment matrix (developed by the Steering Committee) can be presented and commented and/or agreed upon with the other group(s). Areas to compare might be the following with ours:

1. Mission/Vision
2. Foundational principles
3. Strategic objectives
4. Initiatives for the same objective
5. Risk mitigation calculation techniques
6. Performance measurement models
7. Standards, frameworks, and models to be used

Alignment of the strategy must be synchronized with and supportive of the enterprise business objectives. These business objectives can be included in the strategy and a section can describe how they are furthered by the objectives and initiatives of the strategy. These alignments will be discussed again in more detail in STEP 6 as one of the ways of measuring strategic plan performance.

2.2.5 DEVELOPING A STRATEGIC PLAN OVERVIEW REPORTING TEMPLATE

Once the mission/vision, principles, objectives, and initiatives are chosen, an overview template to be used for quarterly or annual reporting purposes can be developed. Shown in Figure 2.7 is an example of a Strategic Plan Reporting template that can be used either for cybersecurity or cyber resiliency.

There will be a more detailed report template presented and discussed in Chapter 7: Measuring Strategic Plan Performance and End of Year (EoY) Tasks.

2.2.6 DETERMINING WORK EFFORTS

Once the Steering Committee members are formalized, tasks to be performed by the Steering Committee can be assigned. The best methodology to be used here is to create a RACI table. Tasks to be performed go on the left, listed downward sequentially, while members (roles) go across the top, from left to right. The RACI table can be used in two separate STEPs:

- STEP 2: Strategy Project Management
  - The Steering Committee creates the initial RACI broken down by the seven STEPs for all the tasks that are necessary to complete for creating and maintaining the strategy

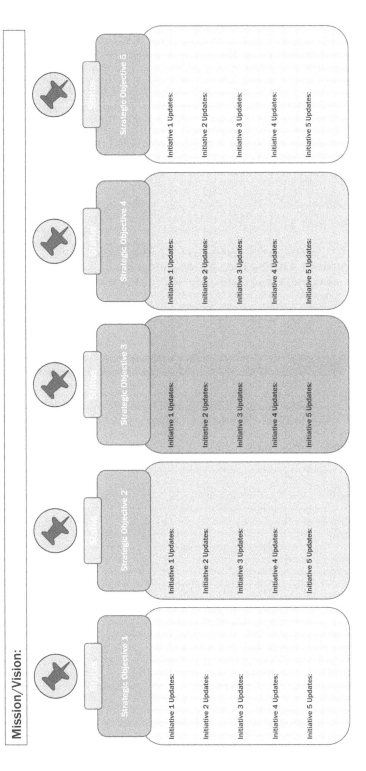

FIGURE 2.7 Strategic Plan Progress Reporting Template for Cybersecurity and Cyber Resiliency.

- STEP 6: Strategic Plan Performance Measurement and EoY Tasks
  - The Steering Committee creates the RACI at the end of the strategy development to list the EoY and yearly tasks that will have to occur going forward once the strategy is approved and operational
  - The Governance RACI can be created to understand the approval critical path

A template is shown in Figure 2.8. The complete RACI chart is filled in for the tasks outlined in all the 6 STEPs of the strategy in detail in Chapter 3: Strategy Project Management.

2.2.7 STRATEGY TIMELINE

The project manager, with input from the Steering Committee can develop a baseline strategy timeline that can show progress on the strategy development to senior management in periodic reports. A sample strategy timeline is shown in Figure 2.9.

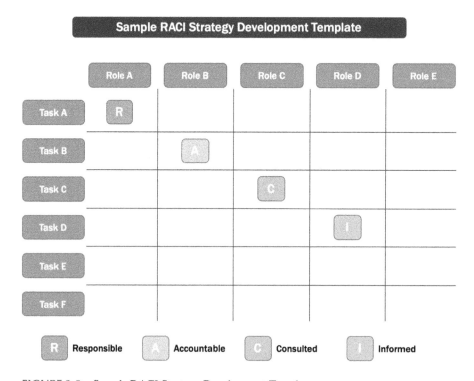

FIGURE 2.8   Sample RACI Strategy Development Template.

FIGURE 2.9 Sample Strategy Timeline.

2.2.8 STRATEGY SWIMLANE

Figure 2.10 shows groups with their interactions and process flows, distinguishing job sharing, and responsibilities for sub-processes for strategy creation and maintenance. Swimlanes are helpful to show the flow of the strategy and how the development process can travel back and forth between groups. A much more detailed swimlane will be presented in Chapter 3: Strategy Project Management showing all the groups that may be involved in the decision-making process.

2.2.9 NIST CSF INITIATIVE MAPPING

As we saw in Chapter 1, one of the most important frameworks for cybersecurity and cyber resiliency is the NIST Cybersecurity Framework, shown again in Figure 2.11. This diagram is referred to multiple times throughout this book. For project

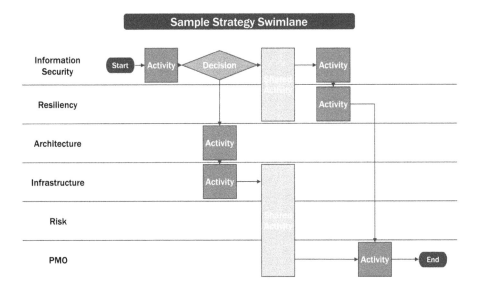

FIGURE 2.10 Sample Strategy Swimlane.

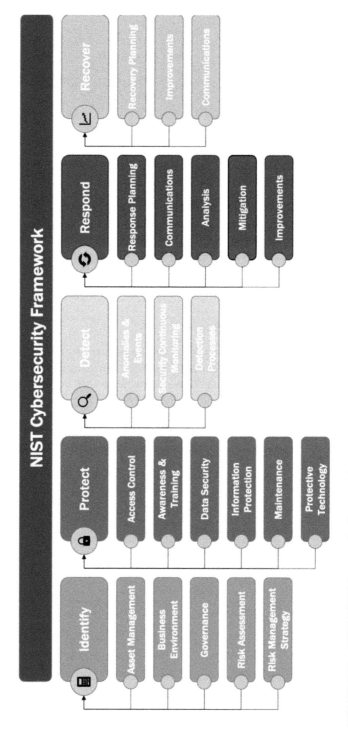

FIGURE 2.11   NIST CSF Cybersecurity Framework.

TABLE 2.19

The Cybersecurity and Cyber Resiliency Strategy Final Deliverable Brief Outline

1. Executive Summary
2. Introduction
3. Cybersecurity and Cyber Resiliency Definitions
4. Steering Group Committee
5. Strategy Purpose and Objectives
6. Methodology for Strategy Development
7. Mission/Vision, Principles, Strategic Objectives, and Cyber Initiatives Identification
8. Strategy Project Management
9. Cyber Threats and Vulnerabilities Analysis
10. Cyber Risks Analysis
11. Cyber Controls Analysis
12. Assessing NIST CSF Current and Target States
13. Cyber Risk and CSF Maturity Rating Assessment Methodologies
14. Measuring Plan Performance
15. Project Reporting
16. EoY Tasks
17. Governance Bodies' Reviews
18. Appendices

management and performance purposes, each of the 5 capabilities will be broken down by the individual initiatives that will support it. In this manner, budgeting and resource balancing can be examined and varying areas of concentration of initiatives will become apparent. In Chapter 3, after the individual initiatives that comprise each of the strategic objectives have been determined, they can be assigned to each of the 5 NIST capabilities.

2.2.10 THE FINAL STRATEGY DOCUMENT DELIVERABLE

The final strategy deliverable document will be comprehensive. Table 2.19 presents a brief listing of the major topics that should be covered. A much more detailed table of contents will be presented in Chapter 3 in Table 3.1, Sample Cybersecurity and Cyber Resiliency Strategy Table of Contents Final Deliverable Outline.

2.3 STEP 3: CYBER THREATS, VULNERABILITIES, AND INTELLIGENCE ANALYSIS

2.3.1 CYBER THREATS

In order to maximize the efficiency and capability of an organization's cybersecurity and cyber resiliency program, threat management plays a significant role. An organization must stay abreast of the current and most destructive threats tailored to the needs and objectives of its people, processes, and technology. The analysis begins with identifying the threat actors.

The most common types of threat actors are:

- Script Kiddies
- Hacktivists
- Organized Crime
- Nation-States
- Insider Threats
- Artificial Intelligence (AI) Powered Threats

Many industry associations and vendors will produce lists of current threats, but it is up to your organization to understand which apply and to what degree – keeping in mind your risk culture and tolerance.

2.3.1.1   Cyber Threat Risk Reporting

In later chapters, formulas, approaches, and methodologies for evaluating risk will be presented which will list some common threats, and assign a rating (1–10), a probability of occurrence (%), and an impact magnitude (1–5). These threat values will be applied to each of the assets: people, processes, and technology. They will then be combined with vulnerability values. The end result will be a relative risk rating for each asset. This is critical to determine as one or more of the assets will be utilized in each of the cybersecurity and cyber resiliency projects.

2.3.2   THREAT INTELLIGENCE, IDENTIFICATION, AND MODELING

Threat intelligence is the act of gaining information on the current cyber threat landscape from a wide worldview. Organizations that can input and analyze cyber threat intelligence effectively can proactively implement measures to reduce their exposure to various threats. Organizations should gather threat intelligence that pertains to their specific area of business.

Threat identification is the process of collecting data on potential threats that can assist management in its identification of cyber security risks. Threat modeling is a structured approach that allows an organization to understand specific threats within a specific network or computer system design.

2.3.3   VULNERABILITIES

A vulnerability refers to any type of weakness in a computer system, an information system, a system security procedure, an internal control, or process, that can be exploited by a threat actor. Below are the main categories of vulnerabilities. They will be gone into more detail in Chapter 4, which will present the Open Web Application Security Project (OWASP) Application Security Vulnerabilities as well.

1. Buffer Overflows
2. Unvalidated Input
3. Race Conditions
4. Access Control Issues
5. Weakness in Authentication, Authorization, or Cryptographic practices

2.3.3.1 Asset Related Vulnerabilities

Assets must have controls protecting them. This in turn will reduce the likelihood of threat exploitation. Cybersecurity programs require that all critical assets have mitigating controls addressing vulnerabilities in the 3 general areas of:

- Prevention
- Detection
- Response

2.3.3.2 Vulnerability Severity Risk Reporting

As was indicated with respect to threats, later chapters will provide formulas, approaches, and methodologies for evaluating risk. These will provide some sample typical vulnerabilities and assign severity ratings (1–5). These vulnerability severity values will be applied to each of the assets: people, processes, and technology. They will then be combined with threat values. The end result will be a relative risk rating for each asset. Again, this is critical to determine as one or more of the assets will be utilized in each of the cybersecurity and cyber resiliency initiatives. The total risk of the initiative can then be derived by understanding the risk of its components.

2.4 STEP 4: CYBER RISKS AND CONTROLS

There are many types of risks. From an organizational view, business risk can be broken down into many components. All are relevant with respect to cybersecurity and cyber resiliency.

2.4.1 Cyber Risk Category Definitions for Business

The following typical business risks should be considered when constructing an enterprise wide cyber risk profile and evaluation approach:

- Information Technology Risk
- Security and Resiliency Risk

- Operational Risk
- Reputational Risk
- Compliance Risk
- Legal Risk
- Program Risk
- Strategic Risk

All of these risks need to be considered within the organization's risk tolerance framework and risk appetite profile.

2.4.2   Risk Appetite and Risk Tolerance

An evaluation of the risk tolerance and risk appetite will set guidelines for the acceptable amount of enterprise risk. Risk appetite is the amount of risk an organization is willing to accept in order to achieve their strategic and business objectives. Risk tolerance is the acceptable level of fluctuation in investment returns that an organization is willing to accept. This level will be derived from and will depend largely on the corporate culture discussed earlier in this chapter.

2.4.3   Cyber Risk Measurement Methodologies

Table 2.20 lists some of the most widely used methodologies. They are explained more in detail in Chapter 5: Cyber Risks and Controls.

2.4.3.1   Cyber Risk Management

There are many definitions of risk management. One defines it as the business risk associated with the use, ownership, operation, involvement, influence, and adoption

---

TABLE 2.20
Risk Measurement Methodologies

1. NIST Special Publication 800-30 Revision 1 (September 2012) is a Guide for Conducting Risk Assessments
2. ISACA Risk Framework – Risk IT[1]
3. The International Organization for Standardization/International Electrotechnical Commission's (ISO/IEC) 27005[2]
4. A Guide to the Project Management Body of Knowledge (PMBOK® Guide)
5. Open Web Application Security Project (OWASP)[3]
6. The Committee of sponsoring Organizations of the Treadway Commission (COSO) 2013 Framework
7. Factor Analysis of Information Risk (FAIR)
8. Carnegie Mellon® Risk Quantification Method (CM RQM)[4]

of IT within an enterprise or organization. Risk management for an organization usually involves most of the following tasks:

- Design and implement a framework and risk governance structure
- Conduct qualitative risk assessments to identify/prioritize key risks
- Quantify all types of risks, including strategic, operational, financial, and insurance
- Develop a clear definition of risk appetite and risk tolerance
- Preform strategic planning
- Involve senior management in implementation and approval of key risks
- Satisfy requirements from rating agencies, regulators, and shareholders

2.4.3.1.1 NIST Cyber Risk Management Framework

US National Institute of Standards and Technology's (NIST) Special Publications 800-37 describes a Risk Management Framework (RMF). The 6 steps of the NIST Risk Management Framework are shown in Figure 2.12.

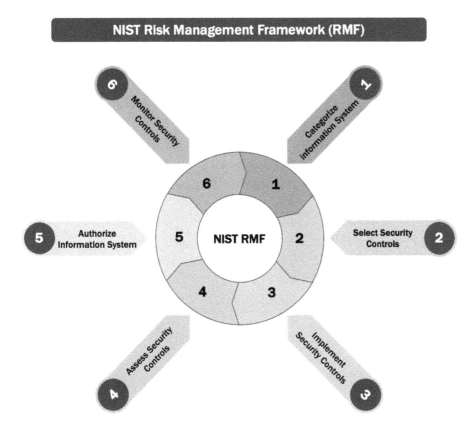

FIGURE 2.12 NIST Risk Management Framework.

The steps are:

1. *Categorize* the system and the information processed, stored, and transmitted by that system based on an impact analysis.
2. *Select* an initial set of baseline security controls for the system based on the security categorization; tailoring, and supplementing the security control baseline as needed based on organization assessment of risk and local conditions.
3. *Implement* the security controls and document how the controls are deployed within the system and environment of operation.
4. *Assess* the security controls using appropriate procedures to determine the extent to which the controls are implemented correctly, operating as intended, and producing the desired outcome with respect to meeting the security requirements for the system.
5. *Authorize* system operation based upon a determination of the risk to organizational operations and assets, individuals, other organizations and the Nation resulting from the operation of the system and the decision that this risk is acceptable.
6. *Monitor* and assess selected security controls in the system on an ongoing basis including assessing security control effectiveness, documenting changes to the system or environment of operation, conducting security impact analyses of the associated changes, and reporting the security state of the system to appropriate organizational officials.

Most risk management standards have common key processes such as:

1. Align enterprise risk management processes to business goals/objectives
2. Identify risks
3. Assess risks
4. Select risk response
5. Monitor risks
6. Communication and report on risk

2.4.3.2 Cyber Risk Calculation

Using the NIST 800-30 SP Rev 1 methodology for quantifying cyber risk, Chapter 5: Cyber Risks and Controls will present a detailed, customized version of a risk assessment of organizational assets such as:

- Human Resources Data – People and Organization
- Network Infrastructure
- Project Management Processes
- Financial – Data Repositories
- E-Commerce – Information Systems
- System Life Cycle Environments
- Cyber Policies, Standards, and Procedures
- Financial Applications
- External/Internet Communications Links

- Business Unit Self-Assessment Processes
- Cybersecurity Software

In Chapter 5: Cyber Risks and Controls, the formula in Figure 2.13 Cyber Risk Score per Asset will demonstrate how an overall risk score can be calculated per asset (people, processes, technology).

A comprehensive spreadsheet will be presented that will calculate the risk score per asset, with explanations on the assignment of the threat, vulnerabilities, probability of occurrence, and impact magnitude rating scales, finishing with the ultimate bucket determination of each asset risk: High, Medium, or Low (H, M, or L).

2.4.4 CONTROLS

Generally speaking, there are two classes of controls:

1. *General Controls:* IT general controls (ITGC) are the basic controls that can be applied to IT systems:
   - Security Administration
   - Data Center Operations
   - Resiliency Management
   - Network Administration
   - Change and Configuration Management
   - Boundary Firewalls and Internet Gateways
   - Access Control and Administrative Privileges

2. *Application Controls:* Application controls are processes and procedures that prevent the application from veering from its intended objective:
   - Application Level Security
   - System Development
   - Change Control
   - Restore and Recovery
   - Secure Configuration
   - Patch Management
   - Malware Protection

The objectives of controls are to ensure the confidentiality, integrity, and availability (CIA) of data, processes, and systems of the organization.

2.4.5 CYBER INSURANCE

Not all risks can be covered through improvements in processes, implementations of technology, or additional training. For organizations that have known risks with no controls, have unknown risks and lack a proper identification and assessment process, or take a risk averse approach to conducting business – cyber insurance could be of benefit. The section on cyber insurance in Chapter 5 will outline the components of cyber insurance policies, what's covered, and additional services provided by insurers that one may not have thought were offered.

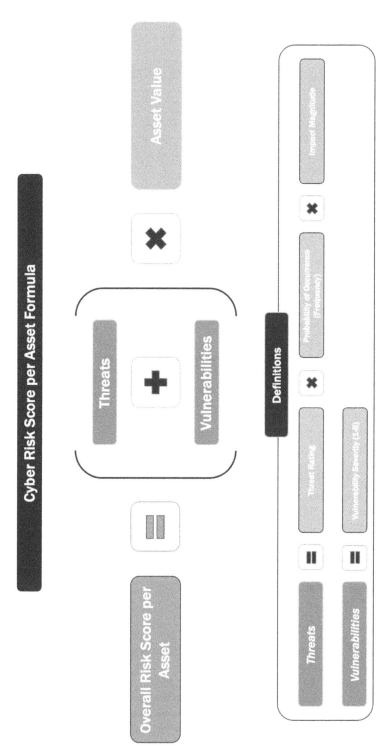

FIGURE 2.13   Cyber Risk Score Per Asset Formula.

2.5 STEP 5: ASSESSING CURRENT AND TARGET STATES

In order to evaluate the current state of cybersecurity and cyber resiliency in one's company, an assessment to determine the baseline and any gaps against a target state should occur.

2.5.1 TYPES OF ASSESSMENTS

There are many types of assessments that can be performed, and Table 2.21 lists some of the most typical types of assessments. What traditionally happens in large organizations, is that multiple areas (please refer back to Chapter 1 where matrixed and siloed organizations are discussed) perform their own assessment. This results in many excessive dollars spent and results that may be incomparable, incompatible, and conflictive in nature. Throughout this section, we will outline the main categories of

---

TABLE 2.21

Assessment Types

Main Categories of Assessment:
  A. Self-Assessments
  B. External/Third-Party Assessments
  C. Audits (Internal & External)

Major Assessment Vehicles: Frameworks, Industry Standards, Regulations, & Models
  1. Frameworks
     a. COBIT (Control Objectives for Information and Related Technologies)
     b. Financial Services Sector Cybersecurity Profile
     c. ISO/IEC 27001
     d. NIST CSF (NIST Cybersecurity Framework)
     e. NIST Risk Management Framework
        • FIPS 199 Categorization
        • NIST 800-53 Control Catalog
     f. CERT©-CRR (Cyber Resilience Review)
     g. COSO ERM Framework
  2. Industry Standards
     a. PCI – DSS (Payment Card Industry – Data Security Standard)
     b. CPMI – IOSCO (Principles for Financial Market Infrastructures [PFMI], Issued by the Committee on Payments and Market Infrastructures and the International Organization of Securities Commissions)
  3. Regulations
     a. NYDFS Cyber Reg. (New York State Department of Financial Services 23 NYCRR 500 Cybersecurity Requirements for Financial Services Companies)
  4. Models
     a. Capability Maturity Model Integration
     b. A Guide to the Project Management Body of Knowledge (PMBOK® Guide)
     c. CERT©-RMM (Resilience Management Model)
     d. Factor Analysis of Information Risk (FAIR)[5] Risk Management Model
     e. Carnegie Mellon® Risk Quantification Method (CM RQM)[4]

---

assessments, what types might be of the most value for certain needs, and some of the most common cybersecurity or cyber resiliency assessment vehicles in the industry.

2.6 STEP 6: MEASURING STRATEGIC PLAN PERFORMANCE AND END OF YEAR (EoY) TASKS

There are many methods of measuring strategic plan performance. Senior management will want some tangible results and some hard metrics to see if the strategy is achieving its goals. First year results may not be comprehensive, as other cyber plans, cyber programs, and cyber initiatives may already be in flight and may be difficult to factor into the overall result. The effect of all these efforts will have a combined result. The strategy should continue on from 4 to 5 years to show definitive and explicit progress. There are a number of ways to measure plan performance – the Steering Committee can select and utilize any or all of the following from the Table 2.22.

All of these measurements should be presented in the final deliverable. A comprehensive final deliverable table of contents will be provided in Chapter 3: Strategy Project Management.

2.6.1 CYBER KEY RISK INDICATORS (KRIs) AND KEY PERFORMANCE INDICATORS (KPIs)

Chapter 7: Measuring Strategic Plan Performance and End of Year (EoY) Tasks goes into detail about how one might create and measure KRIs and KPIs as methods of measuring the strategic plan performance. After the organization decides which risk management framework and measurement approach they wish to deploy, KRIs and KPIs can be developed. Reporting on these quarterly and annually will give senior management a good sense of the strategy's progress. Figures 2.14 and 2.15 are graphical ways of presenting the results.

TABLE 2.22

Sample Methods of Measuring Plan Performance

1. Evaluating the strategy against the critical success factors derived during the strategy planning phase
2. Checking alignment of the strategy with corporate business objectives and other existing corporate strategies
3. Measuring the progress of the individual initiatives/projects that comprise the strategic objectives
4. Noting the improvement in audit, assessment or self-assessment results that are performed at predetermined intervals
5. Showing the decrease in the gap between the current state and the target state
6. The ability to close related audit and/or security findings
7. Utilizing the Key Risk Indicators (KRIs) that have been developed by the enterprise to see if overall risk has decreased and been mitigated
8. Utilizing the Key Performance Indicators (KPIs) that have been developed by the enterprise to see if overall cybersecurity and cyber resiliency has improved

---

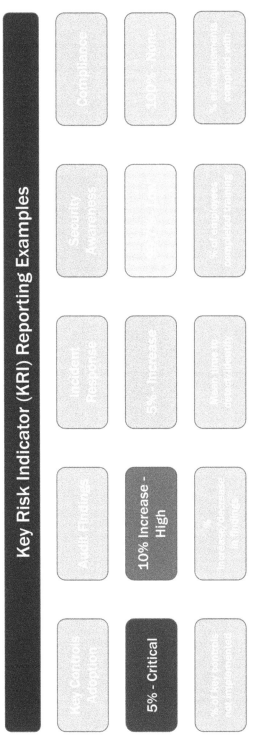

FIGURE 2.14   Cyber Key Risk Indicators Examples.

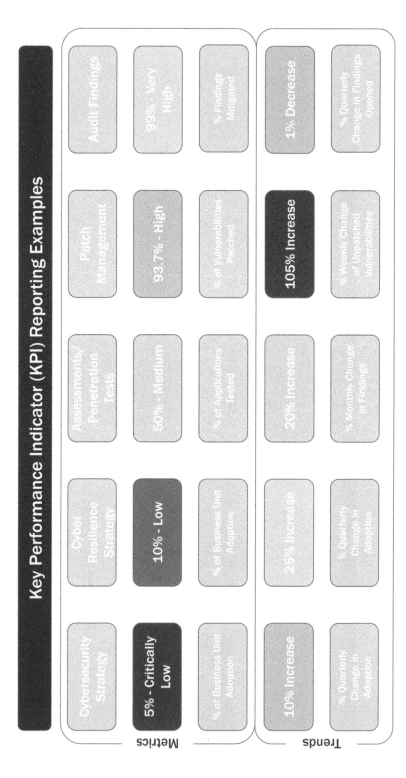

FIGURE 2.15   Cyber Key Performance Indicators Examples.

2.7 GOVERNANCE CYCLES AND PROCESSES

One of the most difficult phases of the strategy approval process is jumping through "governance hoops". Some organizations have extremely complex governance structures and each of those governance bodies may have different authorities with respect to strategy approval. Chapter 7 goes into greater detail into this issue, but for the time being, review the Figure 2.16 and compare it to your organization.

Each of the governance bodies will have different authorities with respect to strategy approval. Some may have review/comment, while some may have approve/reject powers. The best approach is to create a governance body RACI, a sample of which is presented in Chapter 7, and assign roles and responsibilities. In this fashion the PMO assigned to submitting and moving the strategy along the governance critical path will know which bodies are more compulsory and time essential.

It is also suggested that a swimlane be created to understand the flow of the document across and through the governance bodies. A detailed swimlane for the governance bodies above is also presented in Chapter 7, but a sample swimlane is presented earlier in this chapter as Figure 2.10. This will greatly help the PMO in blocking out the appropriate amounts of time to allow for each review, keeping in mind that there may be feedback cycles due to comments that might result in minor or significant changes to the strategy. After these changes, the document may have to proceed along the review path once more time.

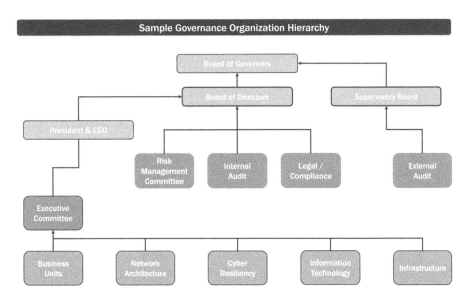

FIGURE 2.16 Sample Governance Organization Hierarchy.

2.8   PROPOSING NEW INITIATIVES TO MITIGATE THREATS AND REDUCE RISK

Determining new initiatives for the following year is an extremely important outcome of the year-end strategy results. This will be discussed in detail in Chapter 7; however, minimally, a number of factors will come into play – namely:

1. The identification of current top threats and vulnerabilities, and their importance to the organization
2. Risk assessment results with respect to assets, people, and technology by internal resources and/or any third party consultancy
3. The resultant KRI and KPI analyses specific to the portfolio of projects (the program) identified by the strategic plans with respect to the official corporate risk tolerance
4. The identification of program concentration gaps of projects/initiatives manifested by the NIST CSF capability assignment analysis
5. The current and actual NIST assessment results with respect to the desired Target State numbers

Methods for deriving each of these performance measurement techniques will be presented and discussed throughout the book. Collectively analyzing these results will identify specific technical areas that may require more attention and resources.

2.8.1   CYBERSECURITY AND CYBER RESILIENCY REPORTING – YEARLY REPORT EXAMPLE

Chapter 7: Measuring Strategic Plan Performance and End of Year (EoY) Tasks will go into detail on how each of the four quadrants of Figure 2.17 can be derived. In this example, the following is shown:

Quadrant #1: For each of the 5 cybersecurity and cyber resiliency strategic objectives, an on track/off track graphic representation is shown.
Quadrant #2: In Chapter 5, a risk assessment methodology is presented. This can be utilized per business unit (BU) per quarter in order to show how risk mitigation is trending.
Quadrants #3 and #4: The 2 graphics on the bottom of the chart show project completion percentages by quarter for each of the 5 initiatives per strategic objective for both cybersecurity and cyber resiliency strategies, clearly indicating their respective progress.

Suffice to say that your organization will have to develop your own personalized cybersecurity and cyber resiliency yearly report, but Figure 2.17 can provide some reporting ideas.

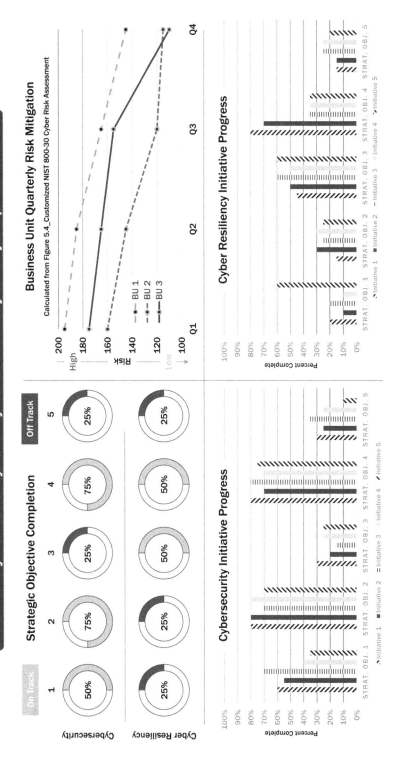

FIGURE 2.17 Sample Cybersecurity and Cyber Resiliency Yearly Report.

2.8.2   REFINING THE STRATEGY OVER TIME – END OF YEAR (EoY) TASKS

Chapter 7: Measuring Strategic Plan Performance and End of Year (EoY) Tasks goes into great detail about what needs to be done toward the end of each year. Here are some of the major tasks.

2.8.2.1   Gathering Data to Measure Strategy Performance

1. Evaluating the strategy against the critical success factors in order to determine the present state
2. Checking alignment of the strategy with corporate business objectives and other existing and/or planned corporate strategies
3. Evaluating the progress of the individual initiatives/projects that comprise the strategic objectives
4. Measuring the improvement in audit, assessment or self-assessment results that are performed at predetermined intervals
5. Measuring the decrease (increase) in the gap between the current state and the target state
6. Utilizing the KRIs and KPIs that have been developed by the enterprise to see if overall risk and performance have decreased (increased)

2.8.2.2   Creating Yearly Reports to Show Performance

1. Generating Current, EoY, and Target State Maturity Tier Ratings using the NIST CSF model
2. Create the Cybersecurity and Cyber Resiliency Yearly Report as shown in the previous section example

2.8.2.3   Determining New Initiatives for the Following Year

The different inputs into developing new initiatives will be further explained in Chapter 7: Measuring Strategic Plan Performance and End of Year (EoY) Tasks, but as a preview, Figure 2.18 is presented to initiate the discussion.

2.8.2.4   Perform Various Project Management Tasks

A number of PMO tasks will have to be completed:

1. Determine the Governance Body Approval Process timeline and critical path
2. Ensure distribution of all Progress Reports to the appropriate parties
3. Confirm Steering Group Members
4. Create a Timeline and draft objectives for the following year

There are more, but they will be presented in Chapter 7: Measuring Strategic Plan Performance and End of Year (EoY) Tasks.

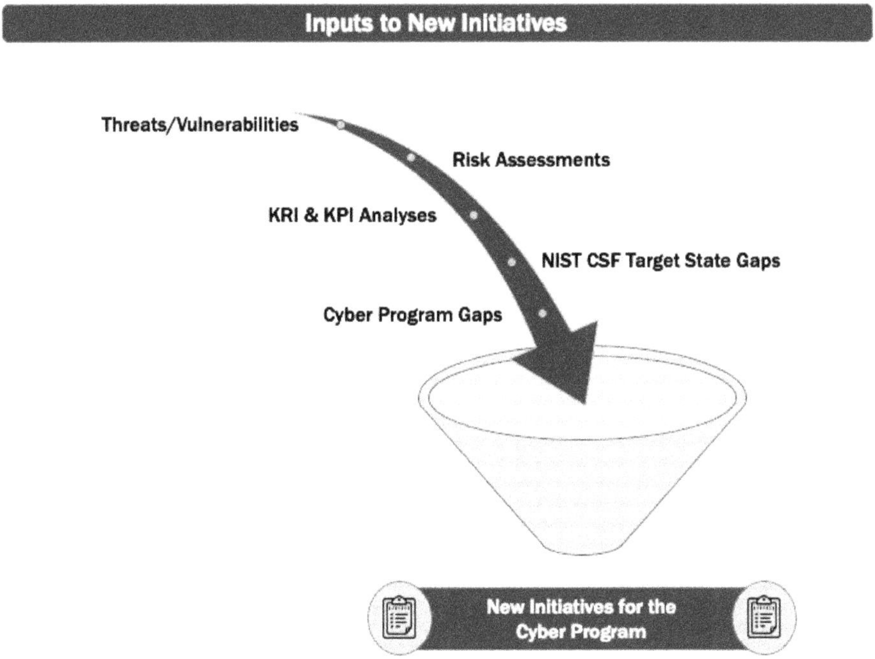

FIGURE 2.18 Inputs to New Initiatives.

2.9 CHECKLISTS AND TEMPLATES

Chapter 8: Checklists and Templates consists of downloadable PDFs of word, excel, and PowerPoint items that have been presented throughout this book. This chapter is meant to aid the reader in using the approaches and methodologies that have been presented and adapting them for their own organizations. In some cases, partial tables, spreadsheets, figures, and diagrams are included so that the reader can fill in the appropriate references for his/her organization. Chapter 8 goes through the 6 STEPs in order and presents the associated figures and data flow diagrams with that STEP. These files in PDF format will be available for download from the CRC Press, Taylor and Francis Group website after purchase of the book.

NOTES

1. Source: The Risk IT Framework ©2009. ISACA. All rights reserved. Used by Permission.
2. ISO/ISEC International Organization for Standardization (ISO) and the International Electrotechnical Commission (IEC).
3. Open Web Application Security Project (OWASP).
4. Carnegie Mellon University, Software Engineering Institute
   - This publication incorporates portions of Technical Report, "Risk Management Framework" by Christopher J. Alberts and Audrey J. Dorofee, CMU/SEI-2010-TR-017 © 2010 Carnegie Mellon University, with special permission from its Software Engineering Institute.

- Any material of Carnegie Mellon University and/or its software engineering institute contained herein is furnished on an "as-is" basis. Carnegie Mellon University makes no warranties of any kind, either expressed or implied, as to any matter including, but not limited to, warranty of fitness for purpose or merchantabiity, exclusivity, or results obtained from use of the material. Carnegie Mellon University does not make any warranty of any kind with respect to freedom from patent, trademark, or copyright infringement.
- This publication has not been reviewed nor is it endorsed by Carnegie Mellon University or its Software Engineering Institute.

5. Source: FAIR Textbook: Measuring and Managing Information Risk, 1st Edition, Published Aug 2014. Permission given by author Jack Freund, PHD, RiskLens.

3 Strategy Project Management

Project management plays a major role in strategy development. The Steering Committee will meet on a regular basis, but it is up to the project manager and the ultimate sponsor of the strategy to drive the agenda, milestones, and deliverables. Each week, there needs to be a certain amount of progress on the final deliverable and it will be up to the project manager to track and show the specific progress as well as to present the items for discussion and consensus.

3.1 VISION TO INITIATIVE FLOW

It is the responsibility of the Steering Committee to define the mission/vision of the strategy. From that vision are born the principles. It is a one-to-many relationship; that is, there can be many principles that apply to the vision. For each principle, there can be many strategic objectives. For each strategic objective, there can be many initiatives/ projects. These too, are both one-to-many relationships as shown in Figure 3.1.

The initiatives may already be ongoing or new ones may have to be launched. There will be a lot of discussion surrounding all of these important decisions so they may take more time than originally allotted. Also, at this time, it will be critical to examine the other strategies in the organization and the overall goals of the organization to ensure that this strategy is in sync with them. Already, some key players from other groups will have been invited to participate in the Steering Committee. Also, here is where the corporate culture comes into play. If the group does not have to fully agree, the decision-making process will move along much faster. If the group has to come to consensus, then it will take a lot longer. It is best to set down guidelines regarding decisions at the beginning of the meetings after the formation of the group; that is for example, if a consensus must be arrived at or if a majority is sufficient.

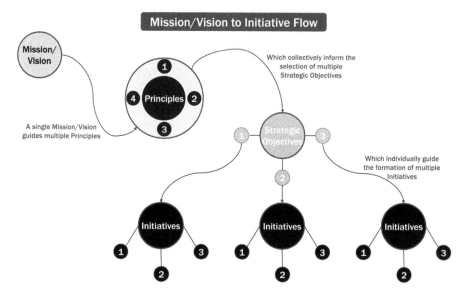

FIGURE 3.1   Mission/Vision to Initiative Flow.

3.2 STRATEGY PROJECT CHARTER

The Steering Committee member from the Project Management Office (PMO) will have to create a Strategy Project Charter in order to officially allocate resources to this project. PMOs use different templates for their project charters, but in Figure 3.2 are some of the essential items that will need to be included in the charter.

3.3 STRATEGY PREPARATION CHECKLIST

Table 3.1 outlines the major steps and decisions that the Steering Group may have to make to initiate the creation of the cybersecurity and cyber resiliency strategies. This is a guide for your organization's preplanning efforts.

3.4 STRATEGY TIMELINE

The Steering Committee together with the PMO can then decide on the overall timeline of the development of the strategy, allowing adequate time for Governance approvals toward the end of the year. In Figure 3.3, a high-level timeline can be developed indicating the tasks of the Steering Committee regarding the development of the strategy. This particular timeline will not show when individual initiatives/projects will be started or finished, but only address the development of the strategy document itself.

Sample Strategy Project Charter

Project Name	Cybersecurity and Cyber Resiliency Strategy		Project Manager	Bill Smith, CISSP
Start Date	CW 1	End Date — CW 50	Project Sponsor	Jane Franklin, VP

Business Need

A unifying cybersecurity and cyber resiliency strategy will allow our organization to develop a risk focused, efficient, and targeted cyber plan

Scope	Deliverables
The development of this cybersecurity and cyber resiliency strategy will cross all organizations and functions within the company	1 Cybersecurity and Cyber Resiliency Strategy that contains: • Mission/Vision • Multiple Principles • Multiple Strategic Objectives • Multiple Initiatives

Potential Risks	Assumptions
If the strategy fails to synthesize across units, or fails to gain executive buy in, the resources spent developing the strategy will be wasted	• Resources will be available • Project will be Approved by Governance Bodies

Schedule

• Please see attached Strategy Gantt Chart and Strategy Timeline

Budget or Resource Commitments

• 2 Full Time SME Employees (FTE) for 40 Calendar Weeks (CW) each
• 1 Full Time Management Employee for 10 CW
• 1 Full Time PMO Employee for 15 CW
• TBD on Oversight, Steering Committee, and Board resource commitments

FIGURE 3.2 Sample Strategy Project Charter.

TABLE 3.1

Strategy Preplanning Checklist

☑ Form a Steering Committee – Designate the key players from top management (see Table 2.1 Steering Committee Members).

☑ Designate the Project Manager for the Steering Committee.

☑ Identify the appropriate SMEs to be included in the Steering Committee.

☑ Agree on corporate culture characteristics, analyze organizational type (Siloed, Matrixed, etc.) – become aware of organization's position on risk (see Figure 2.2 Attributes of Corporate Cultures).

☑ Review Figure 2.5 Organizational Preparation for Cyber Strategy to determine if all the STEPs for strategy development by the organization in general have been executed.

☑ Develop the strategy's critical success factors. These will be used later when evaluating strategy performance.

☑ Start to come to consensus in developing the Steering Committee Tasks. Use the 6 STEPs to organize the tasks.

☑ Present and discuss the corporate business values. Agree that the strategy must incorporate them. They also will be used to evaluate strategy performance.

☑ Determine the overall mission/vision of the strategy. Review Figure 2.6 Mission/Vision, Principles, Strategic Objectives, and Initiatives Pyramid.

☑ Identify the applicable cybersecurity, cyber resiliency, and architectural principles that apply to the strategy.

☑ Gain an understanding of the security and resiliency architectures so that they can be considered when creating the security objectives and initiatives.

☑ Understand all the legal and regulatory guidelines that may apply to the creation and implementation of the strategies.

☑ Derived from the Principles, develop the specific strategic objectives that will achieve the mission of the strategy. Break them down by cybersecurity objectives and cyber resiliency objectives.

☑ For each strategic objective, start to identify the individual initiatives and projects that will achieve each of them. Some will already be in progress.

☑ Perform an enterprise inventory of all cybersecurity and cyber resiliency strategies being planned, in the works, and already published.

☑ Ensure that there is representation of each major effort within the Steering Committee roster.

☑ Develop an alignment matrix that indicates areas of agreement and areas of divergence. This can be included as an Appendix in the final Strategy deliverable.

This timeline is appropriate for presentations to senior management on the high-level tasks of strategy development.

3.5   STRATEGY GANTT CHART

The Gantt Chart is different from the timeline – the timeline is a more high-level deliverable with milestones and is based on the major tasks of the steps of the Steering Committee. The Gantt chart can be laid out by the individual 6 STEPs

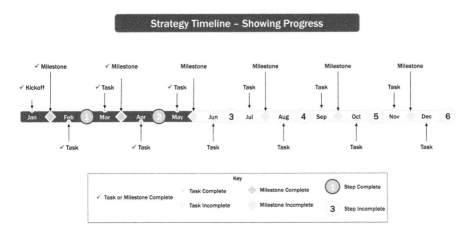

FIGURE 3.3   Strategy Timeline – Showing Progress.

and the individual activities within each step showing a more detailed view of the Steering Committee tasks over the course of one year. Figure 3.4 shows a Gantt Chart template that could be produced by the project manager by hand or a computer application. This could be used by the Steering Committee to see individual STEP progress proceeding throughout the year.

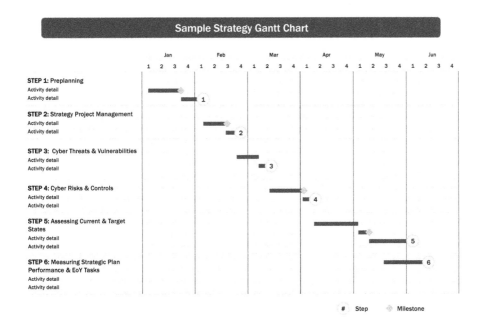

FIGURE 3.4   Sample Strategy Gantt Chart.

3.6 STRATEGY SWIMLANE

The Strategy swimlane is more technical in nature and shows the interaction between areas and outputs of processes during the strategy development and maintenance process. Figure 3.5 is only representative of a generic swimlane – in reality it could be much more complex. This diagram is important, as it shows how multiple groups may be involved in each process, activity or producing a deliverable. It also shows the flow of the strategy development between groups.

3.7 DATA FLOW DIAGRAMS FOR STEPs 2, 3, 4, 5, AND 6

It is helpful to identify all the inputs, outputs, and resources that comprise each of the STEPs. Add any other STEPs specific to your organization. This will aide in sequestering resources and providing critical documentation in a timely manner. Inputs may come from other groups and efforts and may not be a product of the immediate resources of the team. Think far and wide how to provide inputs and resources to the effort, as well as how the results can be the most usefully distributed to gain organizational and political capital for the cause. Inputs, outputs, and resources can be represented by data flow diagrams. The Data Flow Diagrams for STEPs 2–6 are shown in Figures 3.6 through 3.9. These are general diagrams, capturing all the major points. Your organization may require additional inputs, outputs, and/or resources.

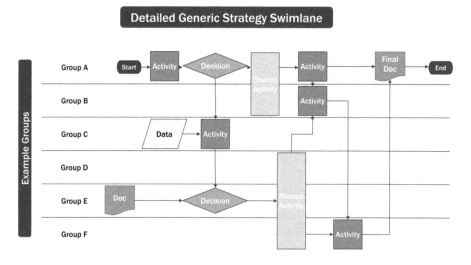

FIGURE 3.5   Detailed Generic Strategy Swimlane.

FIGURE 3.6 Data Flow Diagram for STEP 2: Strategy Project Management.

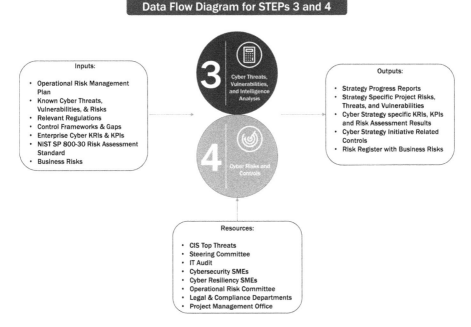

FIGURE 3.7 Data Flow Diagram for STEPs 3: Cyber Threats, Vulnerabilities and Intelligence Analysis and 4: Cyber Risks and Controls.

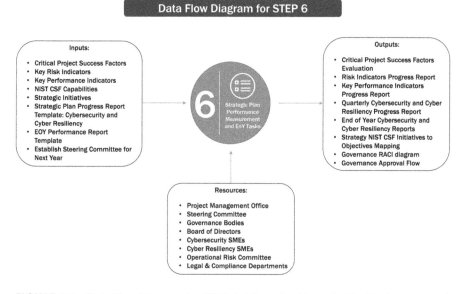

Data Flow Diagram for STEP 5

Inputs:
- General Assessment Process
- Assessment Type Selections
  - Frameworks
  - Industry Standards
  - Regulations
  - Models
- NIST CSF Framework Core Identifiers and Categories
- Cybersecurity and Cyber Resiliency Initiatives Listings
- Maturity Gap Analysis Process with Tier Ratings

5 — Current and Target State Assessments

Outputs:
- Selected Assessments Results
  - Frameworks
  - Industry Standards
  - Regulations
  - Models
- Current & Target State Maturity Gap Analyses' Tier Ratings
- Mapping of Initiatives to the NIST CSF Framework Core Identifiers and Categories
- Relative Initiative Areas of Concentration Revealed
- Listing of Non-Mapped Initiatives and why
- Suggestions for Additional Initiatives

Resources:
- Project Management Office
- Steering Committee
- Cybersecurity SMEs
- Cyber Resiliency SMEs
- Internal/External Audit Comm.
- Legal & Compliance Departments
- Supervisory Comm.
- Operational Risk Committee

FIGURE 3.8 Data Flow Diagram for STEP 5: Assessing Current and Target States.

Data Flow Diagram for STEP 6

Inputs:
- Critical Project Success Factors
- Key Risk Indicators
- Key Performance Indicators
- NIST CSF Capabilities
- Strategic Initiatives
- Strategic Plan Progress Report Template: Cybersecurity and Cyber Resiliency
- EOY Performance Report Template
- Establish Steering Committee for Next Year

6 — Strategic Plan Performance Measurement and EoY Tasks

Outputs:
- Critical Project Success Factors Evaluation
- Risk Indicators Progress Report
- Key Performance Indicators Progress Report
- Quarterly Cybersecurity and Cyber Resiliency Progress Report
- End of Year Cybersecurity and Cyber Resiliency Reports
- Strategy NIST CSF Initiatives to Objectives Mapping
- Governance RACI diagram
- Governance Approval Flow

Resources:
- Project Management Office
- Steering Committee
- Governance Bodies
- Board of Directors
- Cybersecurity SMEs
- Cyber Resiliency SMEs
- Operational Risk Committee
- Legal & Compliance Departments

FIGURE 3.9 Data Flow Diagram for STEP 6: Measuring Strategic Plan Performance and EoY Tasks.

3.8 RACI STRATEGY DEVELOPMENT MATRIX

One of the more important documents produced in STEP 2 is the RACI (Responsible, Accountable, Consulted, Informed) shown in Figure 3.10. This effort is often neglected but is quite important as it spells out all roles and responsibilities, making them clear for the participants and those reading the Strategy.

The RACI represents:

- Members of the Steering Committee
- The STEPs of strategy development and maintenance
- The activities within each step
- The role assigned to each member of the Steering Committee: Responsible, Accountable, Consulted, or Informed (RACI)

Completing this diagram will take a bit of time and full consensus of the Steering Committee, but it will be very useful in identifying the steps, their corresponding tasks, and who has which responsibility. As shown in the swimlane, some tasks may be cross-functional/departmental in nature, and this needs to be determined up front. In the RACI, only one person can be accountable, while multiple persons can have responsibility for the task. The accountable person is the individual who is ultimately answerable for the activity, while the responsible person(s) are those who actually complete the task.

An example of how it might look completely filled in is shown in Figure 3.10a–e.

3.9 NIST CSF INITIATIVE MAPPING

The next step for the Steering Committee is to see how the initiatives map into the NIST CSF diagram. Figure 3.11 is a partial example of how each of the projects/initiatives supports the five capabilities of the NIST CSF model. It is important to see which and how many initiatives contribute to each capability separately in order to determine balance and concentration. It is also important to understand which ones do not map and why.

3.10 THE FINAL STRATEGY DELIVERABLE

As stated before, it is up to the Project Manager and the ultimate Sponsor of the project to drive the creation of the strategy documents. In order to picture how the final deliverable might look, Table 3.2 is provided as a starting point. The contents may vary based on the vision of the Steering Committee. The best method of creating this document is for the project manager to assign sections to different subgroups of the Steering Committee with due dates.

Again, Table 3.2 is only an example. The Steering Group will decide on the contents of the final deliverable.

RACI - CYBERSECURITY AND CYBER RESILIENCY STRATEGY DEVELOPMENT AND MAINTENANCE

STEPS & TASKS		CISO	CTO	CRO	DR/BC	SRM Resiliency	IT Infra	IT Apps	Legal	PMO	Audit	Legal	Compliance	Staff
		STEERING COMMITTEE ROLES												
1	Formalize the Steering Committee members and Project Manager	A,R	R	R	C	C	C	C	I	C	I	I	I	I
2	Agree on the strategy elements: the Pyramid	A,R	R	R	C	C	C	C	I	I	I	I	I	I
3	Create the mission/vision statement	A,R	R	R	C	C	C	C	I	I	I	I	I	I
4	Create the critical success factors	A,R	R	R	C	C	C	C	I	I	I	I	I	I
5	Determine the applicable corporate business values	R	A,R	R	C	C	C	C	I	I	I	I	I	I
6	Agree on corporate culture positioning	A	R	R	I	C	C	C	I	I	I	C	C	I
7	Identify the applicable cybersecurity and cyber resiliency principles	A	R	R	R	R	C	C	I	I	C	C	C	I
8	Create the cybersecurity and cyber resiliency strategic objectives	A	R	R	R	R	C	C	I	I	C	C	C	I
9	Create the cybersecurity and cyber resiliency initiatives	R	A,R	C	R	R	R	R	I	I	I	I	I	C
10	Document the Steering Committee responsibilities	R	A,R	R	R	R	C	C	I	R	C	C	C	I

STEP 1 - PREPLANNING - PREPARATION FOR STRATEGY DEVELOPMENT

(Continued)

FIGURE 3.10   Completed RACI Strategy Development and Maintenance Matrix: a) STEP 1.

RACI - CYBERSECURITY AND CYBER RESILIENCY STRATEGY DEVELOPMENT AND MAINTENANCE

STEERING COMMITTEE ROLES

STEP 2 - STRATEGY PROJECT MANAGEMENT	STEPS & TASKS													
	11	Create the Strategy Project Charter	A-R	R	C	C	C	C	C	R	I	I	I	I
	12	Identify existing and planned cybersecurity and cyber resiliency strategies	A	R	C	C	R	C	I	I	I	I	I	C
	13	Prepare an alignment matrix	A	R	C	C	R	C	I	I	I	I	I	C
	14	Develop a strategy timeline and Gantt chart	A	C	C	C	C	C	R	I	I	I	C	I
	15	Develop a strategy swimlane	A-R	C	C	C	C	C	R	C	C	C	C	I
	16	Create the operational RACI for all the Steering Committee tasks	A-R	C	C	C	C	C	R	C	C	C	C	I
	17	Map the initiatives to the NIST CSF	A-R	C	R	R	R	C	R	C	C	C	C	I
	18	Create outline of final strategy deliverable	A-R	R	R	C	C	C	R	C	C	C	C	I

FIGURE 3.10 (Continued) Completed RACI Strategy Development and Maintenance Matrix: b) STEP 2.

(Continued)

RACI - CYBERSECURITY AND CYBER RESILIENCY STRATEGY DEVELOPMENT AND MAINTENANCE

STEERING COMMITTEE ROLES

STEPS & TASKS	CISO	CTO	CRO	DR-BC	Bus. Resiliency	IT Apps	IT Infra	Fraud	PMO	Audit	Legal	Compliance	SME
19 Determine the current business threats in priority order	A,R	R	R	R	R	R	R	C	I	C	C	C	C
20 Determine the current business vulnerabilities in priority order	A,R	R	R	R	R	R	R	C	I	C	C	C	C
21 Analyze the process for current threat intelligence	R	A,R	R	C	R	R	R	C	I	C	C	C	C
22 Acknowledge enterprise risk tolerance and risk appetite standards and apply to the strategy	R	R	A,R	C	C	C	C	I	I	I	I	C	C
23 Agree on a risk measurement methodology or accept the corporate standard	R	R	A,R	C	C	C	C	I	I	C	I	I	C
24 Create the Cyber Key Risk Indicators (KRI) and Key Performance Indicators (KPI)	R	R	A,R	C	C	C	C	I	I	C	I	I	C
25 Take an inventory on how controls are implemented and monitored	R	R	R	C	C	A	C	I	I	R	C	R	C
26 Correlate risks, threats and vulnerabilities to controls	R	R	A,R	C	R	C	C	I	I	R	I	C	C

STEP 3 - CYBER THREATS, VULNERABILITIES & INTELLIGENCE ANALYSIS

STEP 4 - CYBER RISKS & CONTROLS

(Continued)

FIGURE 3.10 (Continued) Completed RACI Strategy Development and Maintenance Matrix: c) STEPs 3 and 4.

RACI - CYBERSECURITY AND CYBER RESILIENCY STRATEGY DEVELOPMENT AND MAINTENANCE

STEERING COMMITTEE ROLES

STEPS & TASKS		CISO	CTO	CIO									
STEP 5 - ASSESSING THE CURRENT & TARGET STATES	27	Inventory all cyber related assessments past, present and future	R	R	R	C	R	C	C	A	C	I	C	I
	28	Evaluate and decide on assessment types to be used in determining current & target states	A,R	C	R	C	R	C	I	I	I	I	I	C
	29	Decide on which assessment types will be recognized/adopted	R	A,R	R	C	R	C	I	I	C	C	C	C
	30	Create assessment schedules to determine future plan performance	R	A,R	R	C	R	C	I	I	C	C	C	C
	31	Agree on the high level cyber program	R	A,R	R	R	R	C	C	I	I	I	I	C
	32	Agree on the adoption of NIST CSF for the main cyber framework	A,R	C	C	C	C	I	I	R	I	I	C	C
	33	Assess current and target states	A,R	R	R	R	R	I	I	I	C	I	C	R

FIGURE 3.10 (Continued) Completed RACI Strategy Development and Maintenance Matrix: d) STEP 5.

(Continued)

RACI – CYBERSECURITY AND CYBER RESILIENCY STRATEGY DEVELOPMENT AND MAINTENANCE

STEP 6 – MEASURING STRATEGIC PLAN PERFORMANCE & EOY TASKS

STEPS & TASKS	CISO	CIO	CHRO	DPO/BSO	Bus. Resiliency	IT mngt	IT Arch	user	PMO	Legal	Compliance	SME
34 Complete the yearly strategy progress report	A,R	R	R	C	C	–	–	–	R	I	C	C
35 Ensure compliance with regulations	A	R	R	R	R	R	R	C	R	C	C	I
36 Prepare the EoY Strategy Performance Measurement Plan (KRIs, KPIs) and Critical Success Factors metrics	A,R	R	R	C	C	C	C	–	R	C	C	R
37 Determine corporate governance requirements	A,R	R	R	–	–	–	–	–	R	C	C	I
38 Schedule reviews with governance bodies	R	R	R	–	–	–	–	–	A	C	C	I
39 Distribute EoY reports to senior management	A,R	I	–	–	–	–	–	–	R	I	I	I
40 Create additional strategy performance reports	A,R	C	C	C	C	C	C	–	–	I	–	C
41 Establish objectives for the following year	A,R	R	R	C	C	C	C	–	–	I	–	C
42 Create list of possible new initiatives for following year	A,R	R	R	R	R	R	R	C	R	I	I	R
43 Confirm Steering Group Committee member composition going forward	A,R	C	C	C	C	C	C	C	–	C	C	I
44 Create timeline for following year	A	R	C	–	–	–	–	–	R	I	C	I

FIGURE 3.10 (Continued)   Completed RACI Strategy Development and Maintenance Matrix: e) STEP 6.

Sample NIST CSF to Initiative Mapping

CSF Capability	Initiative	CSF Capability	Initiative
Identify	Develop a standard cyber hygiene approach by implementing critical security controls	Protect	Segment the technical architecture according to risk level
Identify	Evaluate supply chain chokepoints for IT services and understand critical 3rd party services	Protect	Advertise elements of the Cybersecurity Awareness program on the premises of the organization as well as online
Identify	Develop a Cybersecurity Awareness Program	Detect	Develop and implement a comprehensive asset protection program consisting of asset, vulnerability, patching, logging, monitoring, and alerting modules for the complete inventory of all technology assets
Identify	Perform a threat analysis for critical systems and high risk areas	Detect	Create a cyber threat intelligence program that collects and analyzes current threat information regarding cyber attacks in order to contribute to the overall asset risk calculation
Identify	Perform a risk assessment to quantify the current state	Respond	Create a plan for dual site failover and recovery
Identify	Develop a list of critical systems, applications, and businesses in priority order	Respond	Participate and collaborate in industry-wide cyber resiliency and industry and gaming events
Identify	Implement a 24/7 Incident Response Team inclusive of digital forensics	Respond	Develop a list of critical systems, applications and businesses in priority order
Identify	Document all cyber business risks and responses within a risk register	Recover	Issue an RFI and select a breach response vendor

FIGURE 3.11 Sample NIST CSF Initiative Mapping.

TABLE 3.2

Sample Cybersecurity and Cyber Resiliency Strategy Table of Contents (TOC) Final Deliverable Outline

1. Introduction
2. Executive Summary
3. Scope and Objectives of the Strategies
4. Cybersecurity and Cyber Resiliency Definitions
5. Steering Group Committee
    5.1 Members and Responsibilities
    5.2 Committee Charter
    5.3 RACI Strategy Development Template Chart
    5.4 Corporate Culture and Organizational Analysis
    5.5 Critical Success Factors
    5.6 Business Goals
    5.7 Risk Appetite
6. Purpose and Objectives of the Cybersecurity and Cyber Resiliency Strategies
    6.1 Defining the Mission/Vision Pyramid
    6.2 Principles
    6.3 Strategic Objectives
    6.4 Initiatives/Projects
    6.5 NIST CSF Mapping of Initiatives to Capabilities to Strategic Objectives
7. Methodology for Strategy Development
    7.1 The 6 STEPs for Cybersecurity and Cyber Resiliency Strategy Development
        7.1.1 STEP 1: Preplanning: Preparation for Strategy Development
        7.1.2 STEP 2: Strategy Project Management
        7.1.3 STEP 3: Cyber Threats, Vulnerabilities, and Intelligence Analysis
        7.1.4 STEP 4: Cyber Risks and Controls
        7.1.5 STEP 5: Current and Target State Assessments
        7.1.6 STEP 6: Strategic Plan Performance Measurement and EoY Tasks
8. Strategy Project Management
    8.1 Project Charter
    8.2 High-Level Timeline with Milestones and Progress
    8.3 Full Project Gantt Chart
    8.4 Strategy Development Project Swimlane
    8.5 Initiatives per Strategic Objective
    8.6 Sample NIST CSF Initiative Mapping
    8.7 Full Project RACI by Steering Committee member showing tasks and responsibilities for each of the 6 STEPs
9. Cyber Threats and Vulnerabilities Analysis
    9.1 Types of Cyber Threats
    9.2 Assessing Vulnerabilities
    9.3 Types of Cyber Attacks
10. Cyber Risk Analysis
    10.1 Types of Cyber Risks
    10.2 Risk Appetite and Risk Tolerance
    10.3 Cyber Risk Measurement Methodologies
    10.4 NIST 800-30 Cyber Risk Measurement Spreadsheet

(Continued)

TABLE 3.2 *(Continued)*

Sample Cybersecurity and Cyber Resiliency Strategy Table of Contents (TOC) Final Deliverable Outline

11. Cyber Controls Analysis
    11.1 Types of Cyber Controls
    11.2 Mapping of Threats/Vulnerabilities to Risks and Controls
    11.3 Cyber Insurance
12. Assessing NIST CSF Current and Target States
    12.1 Standards and Frameworks Used
    12.2 Methodologies and Metrics for Assessments
    12.3 NIST 800-30 Cyber Risk Measurement Methodology
    12.4 NIST CSF Assessment Measuring Current and Target State
    12.5 Discussion of Mapped and Un-Mapped Initiatives
    12.6 Maturity Rating Methods
13. Measuring Plan Performance
    13.1 Developing Cyber Key Risk Indicators (KRIs)
    13.2 Developing Cyber Key Performance Indicators (KPIs)
    13.3 Comparisons against:
        13.3.1 Business Objectives
        13.3.2 Critical Success Factors
        13.3.3 KRIs and KPIs
        13.3.4 Strategy Alignment
        13.3.5 Audit/Security findings closed
14. Project Reporting
    14.1 Yearly Strategy Performance Reports
    14.2 Project Progress per Strategic Objective
    14.3 Risk Mitigation by Business Unit
    14.4 Current and Target States Maturity Tier Rating
15. End of Year Tasks
    15.1 Steering Committee Members for the next year
    15.2 RACI for the next Year
    15.3 Proposing New Initiatives
16. Governance Review
    16.1 Ensuring Compliance with Regulations
    16.2 Governance Review Bodies and corresponding RACI
    16.3 Timeline for Governance Review
    16.4 Organizational Swimlane for Governance Review
17. Appendices
    17.1 Full RACI for Complete Project
    17.2 Strategy Alignment Matrix

4 Cyber Threats, Vulnerabilities, and Intelligence Analysis

Corporate cybersecurity and cyber resiliency plans must address viable threats and vulnerabilities in order to be successful. Robust Threat Awareness and Vulnerability Management programs are key in order to elevate the maturity posture of an organization. In order to maximize the efficiency and the capabilities of their cybersecurity and cyber resiliency programs, an organization must understand the roles that threat management and vulnerability management play and the outputs these programs provide. Proper threat management allows an organization to understand the threats within the world economy, within the surrounding industry, and those relevant to the organization. Proper vulnerability management will then allow the organization to limit its exposure to worldwide threats, industry-wide threats, and, most importantly, its exposure to threats that target the organization. It is also urgent to have a timely vulnerability and patch management program. As incident after incident has shown, the time from alert to attack can be short – and proper vulnerability (and patch) management is key to make the most of precious days, or even hours. Figure 4.1 shows a generalized picture of how threats target security organizations and compromise assets which, ideally, are protected by security policies and controls.

The assets, on the far right of the diagram, are both the "crown jewels" of the organization as well as the main target for the threat actors on the left side of the diagram. Threat actors will study an environment or organization for as long as possible, and it is up to the security organization to develop the appropriate policies and controls to mitigate these threats to their key assets.

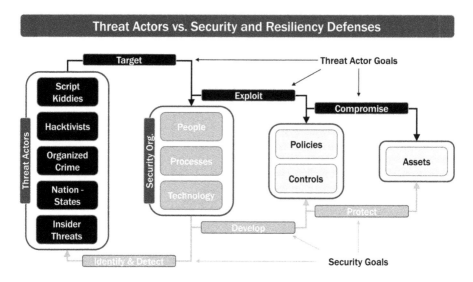

FIGURE 4.1   Threat Actors vs. Security and Resiliency Defenses.

4.1   THREATS IN THE CONTEXT OF A CYBERSECURITY AND CYBER RESILIENCY STRATEGY

A threat awareness program and proper inter-communication provide organizations intelligence related to what outcomes are possible – not how outcomes will occur. The threats that organizations are facing today are highly developed and growing in magnitude as well as quantity. From an enterprise-wide perspective, it is up to the organization to determine what threats exist, what threats are relevant, and which threats are the most pressing. The final objective is to mitigate the associated risks of those threats. While industry groups, such as the Financial Services Information Sharing and Analysis Center (FS-ISAC), may assist with determining what threats exist, it rests solely on the organization itself to develop adequate responses to their threats. A mature organization will develop a cybersecurity and cyber resiliency program that is tailored to the particular threats facing their organization. Organizations that fail to take a threat-driven approach and, instead, choose to rely on outdated and simplistic approaches to cybersecurity and cyber resiliency program management will:

- Waste limited resources on areas that may not be relevant
- Accept inefficiencies in their programs
- Suffer a culture of response latency

Mature organizations use models to guide their threat management program and recommended processes to produce meaningful outputs for decision makers. A strategy that incorporates threat management within an organization's cybersecurity and cyber resiliency programs is mandatory. Mature organizations that have a heavy reliance on vendors or upstream suppliers should also incorporate the threat management of their suppliers/vendors into their strategy.

4.1.1 Definition of a Threat

According to the National Institute of Standards and Technology's SP-800-30, a threat is any circumstance or event with the potential to create loss. While there is an endless amount of possible threats to a business, in the context of cyber, a cyber threat is the possibility of a malicious actor attempting to damage or disrupt a computer network or system. So, combining the two definitions allows us to come up with the basic definition of a cyber threat – any circumstance or event with the potential to create loss by damaging or disrupting a computer network or system.

4.1.2 Evolution of Cyber Threats

The growth and proliferation of cyber threats over the recent years should not come as any surprise. As the Internet became an increasingly integral aspect of modern business, many IT systems were placed within easy and unmanaged access of the open Internet. Over the years, the cybersecurity industry has grown and increased the maturity of its product offerings. However, it has not been enough. There is one thing that we can determine for sure about cybercrime – it is not going away and will continue to become more sophisticated and dangerous. Cyber threats have further evolved as global business has become exponentially more technology dependent. For example, some of the largest cyber threats of the past involved a pure data breach scenario, and this was fairly straightforward – various companies had massive databases of personal information with loose security controls and poorly followed processes protecting this data. It should come as no surprise that what followed were massive data breaches. The companion domain of this book – Cyber Resiliency – was not the original focus of the security organization or business leaders. However, this changed with the advent of rapidly spreading and self-replicating malware and the ability to cripple an organization's operations. Highly publicized attacks using this vector have altered the way businesses think about protecting their operations. This shows that whatever the intent behind the attacks, whether malicious or otherwise, cybercrime has become big business.

4.1.2.1 The Early Stages of Cyber Threats

It is nearly impossible to put a date on the first established cyber threat, but one would have to imagine that not long after computers were first connected did the temptation exist for nefarious activity. This mindset continues today as the basic premise of a cyber threat remains unchanged: someone has something the other person wants, wants to manipulate, or wants to destroy. As was alluded above, the early stages of cyber threat focused on breaches of confidentiality and bravado.

4.1.2.2 Present-Day and Future Cyber Threat Actors

As information systems become more and more connected, cyber threat actors have a plethora of options to gain a foothold into any company. The convergence of operational technology (OT), traditional business processes, Internet of Things (IoT) devices, and the expansion of cloud computing will enable businesses to collect troves of data and maximize efficiencies within their processes. However, as the opportunity for businesses to increase manufacturing production, maximize data collection, and implement a scalable computing infrastructure increases, more and more devices are connected to the internet, particularly in ways that may be vulnerable. This results in a substantial increase in the impact and likelihood of a cyberattack. Threat actors are aware of this, and there have been many high-profile incidents of great loss as organizations were not aware of the possible consequences of having many OT or SCADA systems connected to one another with minimal controls in place. Although the threat landscape appears to be trending in the direction of impacting companies with highly integrated networks that overlap between traditional IT and OT, all is not lost. The benefits of integrating these IT and OT networks, connecting multitudes of IoT devices, or outsourcing business processes to computing power contained in the cloud, can all be had as long as the organization is aware of the associated threats that each individual landscape brings with it. For a bit of time, cloud computing was seen as the cure-all for the modern organization. The Software as a Service (SaaS) and Infrastructure as a Service (IaaS) models were thought to simply allow companies to rid themselves of the issues of cybersecurity. The thought, incorrectly, was that service providers would be handling all of the security. As breach after breach has shown, utilizing cloud computing resources has turned out to be no more secure – and when not understood, configured, and managed properly, less secure than standard, in-house IT operations. However, it should be noted that utilizing a properly designed, configured, and managed cloud computing environment can be a good way to increase cyber resiliency maturity.

Another trend that is increasing and troubling executives is the threat of malware and ransomware. Malware and ransomware are elaborated upon in Section 4.3. They are serious cyber threats that can impact both the security and resiliency domains. This kind of attack is generally a result of a security failure that has the potential to halt an organization's business processes or manufacturing, and potentially eradicate the organization's data and backups.

Lastly, another trend that is worrisome is the fact that most cyberattacks are not reported, or if they are reported, the impact of the attack is understated. A few reasons for this are as follows:

- Some areas do not have breach reporting laws
- Areas that do have breach reporting laws may only require the notification if Personally Identifiable Information (PII) is impacted
- Less mature organizations believe that quietly settling a breach is the best way to minimize negative impacts

As Table 4.1 outlines, modern-day and advanced persistent threat (APT) threat actors have developed ways to penetrate even the most well-defended network perimeters by exploiting distinct advantages that the modern threat actors have.

Today and in the future, cyber threat actors will exploit some of our greatest technological advances. One can say this with confidence, due to the great faith that, as risk management professionals, we have confidence in nefarious actors likely succeeding. It's important to remember that, just as today, future cyber defenses must work 100% of the time, while future cyber threat actors (offenders) only have to work

TABLE 4.1

Modern Threat Advantages for the Attacker

1. There is no 100% effective way to prevent zero-day vulnerabilities from being exploited.
2. There is no method to patch software as soon as vulnerabilities are discovered.
3. There is no 100% and cost-effective method of securing supply chains and dependent operations.
4. There is no sure-fire way of preventing employees from becoming insider threats.
5. Training and awareness programs are not 100% effective at mitigating vulnerabilities within human-based processes.

once to have their respective actions deemed a success. This is a point that cannot be reiterated enough – most breaches are caused by small mishaps and oversights within the security posture of an organization.

4.1.3 TYPES OF THREATS AND ACTORS

The types of cybersecurity and cyber resiliency threats vary widely. Within the realm of cyber threat capabilities, the quality of the threat is dependent upon the training and resources – the backing that the threat actor has. What is important to discern from the following sections is that as the training of the threat actors within groups increases, the likelihood of a successful attack increases. The most high-profile organizations must realize that they are a target of all cyber threat actors and should equip their programs aggressively. It is important to note that the list provided below is by no means an exhaustive list and should be considered a starting point. One of the most important aspects of having a cyber threat awareness capability is the understanding that the threat landscape is constantly evolving – a threat today is not necessarily a threat tomorrow. But even more important to understand is that calm today does not guarantee calm tomorrow. Figure 4.2 lists some of the most common threat actors.

4.1.3.1 Script Kiddies

Script kiddies, the most comically represented members of the cyber threat actor group, are somewhat as they sound – they are low-level individuals or groups that partake in hacking for experimentation purposes or for low-level crimes. While they are rarely successful at infiltrating the defenses of the largest and most well-funded targets – Financial Services, Government, Health Care – attacks most commonly attributed to script kiddies constitute the largest quantity of attacks.

4.1.3.2 Hacktivists

Hacktivists are a group that blends the lines between social activism and for-profit hacking. These skilled threat actors use technology to promote a political agenda or to cause social change; usually related to freedom of speech, freedom of information, or human rights. Hacktivism is quite controversial, as the groups and individuals representing the hacktivist community span the entire political spectrum. Hacktivists are generally very highly skilled, very mature, and lie within an area

FIGURE 4.2   Threat Actors.

that should be of great concern for any organization. The reputational and financial losses that can occur from a hacktivist attack are nothing to take lightly. While these groups may not be targeting financial bounties, they may be targeting organizations and their associated websites as pawns in their missions to cause political protest.

4.1.3.3   Organized Crime Groups

Organized crime groups are generally highly skilled and toward the more mature end of the cyber threat actor spectrum. These threat actors have a concentration in the areas concerning fraud and monetary theft. Cyberattacks attributed to these groups may not be headline grabbing but could fall just below the radar as to allow their attacks to persistently attempt fraudulent transactions or steal data/balances of a monetary value. Also remember that organizations often choose not to publicize their breaches.

4.1.3.4   Nation-States

Nation-States are generally the most mature and most advanced of all the threat actors. Their purpose is largely to conduct cyber warfare against enemy territories or organizations representative of enemy territories. Nation-State actors, for the most part, have seemingly unlimited budgets, highly skilled teams, and motivation rested in national pride. Cyberattacks attributed to Nation-State actors are generally highly

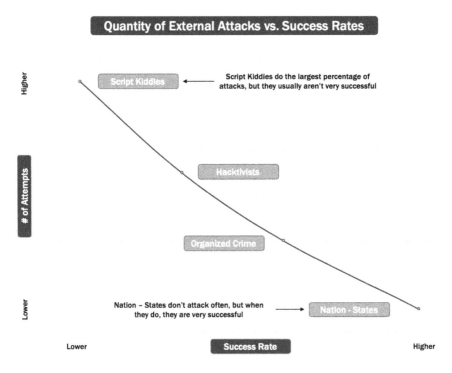

FIGURE 4.3 Quantity of External Attacks vs. Success Rates.

targeted, extremely complex in nature, and require the best defenses to even notice their footprints. Financial Services companies, Government agencies, defense contractors, and similar organizations are the most likely subjects.

While all threat actors are successful some of the time, Nation-States are the most successful of the list. As shown in Figure 4.3, there is actually an inverse relationship between the quantity of external attacks and their success rates due to the increasing sophistication of the threat actor.

4.1.3.5 Insider Threats

Insider threats are a completely separate breed of cyber threats. While the insider threat is not something new, the processes by which insider threats are carrying out their attacks are changing in the cyber age. Insider threats, as the name suggests, are threats from within the organization. These threats are particularly troubling due to the fact that the very nature of these threats places them within the organizational boundaries – all external defenses are usually rendered useless when protecting against insider threats.

4.1.3.6 Artificial Intelligence Powered Threats

Artificial Intelligence (AI), sometimes called machine language, is an area of computer science that deals with giving machines the ability to copy intelligent human behavior. AI enables cybercriminals to breach security systems in a variety of ways being able to mutate itself as it learns about the environment. Below are 3 types of contemporary AI malware attacks.

1. Adversarial AI Attacks
   In this case attackers can perform cryptocurrency mining malware. In this case, processing power is stolen to perform digital currency mining (e.g., bitcoin).
   Another example is the use of AI to impersonate users, copying their writing style, enabling them to target specific individuals.
2. The Emotet Trojan
   The Emotet Trojan attack can self-propagate, using brute-forcing passwords and spam modules. Emotet is downloaded and then executes a spreader module that the victim is unaware of. In these cases, clicking on a link or downloading a malicious attachment are not required.
3. Model Inversion
   In this case, adversaries basically reverse-engineer the machine learning (ML) of a model and its respective algorithms, thereby altering the result. This particular type of attack has major privacy concerns.

4.1.4 THREAT INTELLIGENCE, IDENTIFICATION, AND MODELING

Threat intelligence is the act of gaining information on the current cyber threat landscape from a wide worldview. Organizations that can input and analyze cyber threat intelligence effectively can proactively implement measures to reduce their exposure to various threats. Threat identification is the process of collecting data on potential threats that can assist management in its identification of information security risks. Threat modeling is a structured approach that allows an organization to understand specific threats within a specific network or computer system design. Threat modeling involves building scenarios that reflect possible events. Each asset is analyzed from the perspective of the impact (liability) of various threats scenarios. Examples of impact produced by threats include:

- Direct costs from physical destruction/loss
- Direct costs from theft and/or extortion
- Costs to resolve incidents (internal productivity loss, outside resources)
- Loss of consumer confidence
- Failure to meet regulatory requirements
- Failure to meet contractual agreements
- Worst case scenarios (catastrophic failures of information systems that result in physical destruction, death, injury, or an inability to continue operations)

The scenarios listed above can only happen if a threat impacts an asset that has a vulnerability – known or unknown. The asset and threat information collected indicate possible areas of impact to the business. However, the likelihood of these impacts then need to be determined, thus yielding the final components used to perform a risk assessment. Chapter 5: Cyber Risks and Controls will review typical types of risks, their corresponding controls, and provide an actual risk assessment using the NIST 800-30 model. Chapter 6: Current and Target State Assessments will discuss the most widely used types of risk assessments and how they can be used to evaluate corporate maturity levels and gaps.

4.1.4.1 MITRE ATT&CK

MITRE's Adversarial Tactics, Techniques, and Common Knowledge (ATT&CK) model is a model for cyber adversary behavior, which reflects the various phases of an adversary's attack life cycle and the platforms they are known to target. Per the MITRE[1] Group, "The basis of ATT&CK is the set of individual techniques that represent actions that adversaries can perform to accomplish objectives. Those objectives are represented by the tactic categories the techniques fall under. This relatively simple representation strikes a useful balance between sufficient technical detail at the technique level and the context around why actions occur at the tactic level." One of the more interesting concepts about the MITRE ATT&CK methodology is that the methodology is adversary focused and maintains the adversary's perspective. Contrast this with most security methodologies and models that describe desired cybersecurity and cyber resiliency activities from the defender's perspective.

The MITRE ATT&CK[2] behavioral model is comprised of the following:

- Tactics
- Techniques
- Adversary Usage

Tactics denote short-term, tactical adversary goals during an attack while techniques describe the means by which adversaries achieve tactical goals. Adversary usage is documented usage of techniques. Table 4.2 can be helpful for creating a threat and intelligence management program.

4.1.4.2 Threat Intelligence, Identification, and Modeling within a Strategy and a Program

In the context of a cybersecurity or cyber resiliency strategy, threat intelligence is one of the foundational aspects. Threat intelligence is used as an input within the strategy to understand what nefarious actors require the defenses provided by the

---

TABLE 4.2

MITRE ATT&CK Use Cases[3]

1. Adversary Emulation
2. Red Teaming
3. Behavioral Analytics Development
4. Defensive Gap Assessment
5. SOC Maturity Assessment
6. Cyber Threat Intelligence Enrichment

---

security program. The threat intelligence program shapes the outputs of the cyber-security and cyber resiliency program. This action of tailoring the cyber program, and the associated strategy, to the relevant threats the organization faces allows the organization to be aware and efficient. Threat intelligence is a pillar within the risk-driven strategic process.

Often times, third parties are brought in to conduct threat intelligence and evaluate the threat landscape. Many security companies offer threat intelligence as a service. If an organization possesses the capability to conduct threat intelligence internally, the reports should not be created in a vacuum – members of the cyber-security and/or cyber resilience teams should be interviewed to gain feedback on the reports. For example, if a specific threat actor group is targeting a vulnerability within a brand and model of network switches, the manager of the particular group responsible for these network components should be interviewed to determine if the threat scenario is likely, what the associated impact would be if the threat were to target the organization, and whether or not there are any compensating controls in place to mitigate the risk. This feedback should also be discussed one-on-one with a manager who is not in the direct reporting line.

Furthermore, there are many organizations that produce threat intelligence information that are available to corporations. These should be reviewed. There are also groups of business organizations that discuss threats on a regular basis. All these avenues of gathering intelligence should be considered and deployed.

When looking at threat intelligence from an aggregate level, there must be continued dialogue between business representatives, cybersecurity, cyber resilience, and IT management and personnel as well as those who oversee the day-to-day operations of business processes. This is crucial to ensure that the organization can strategize cohesively to take the correct action in response to the threats.

4.1.4.3 Monitoring for Threats

Threat monitoring is where all the prework of establishing a threat management model pays off. Holistic threat models use the outputs of threat monitoring exercises and programs as inputs into their models, which then become inputs into the overall cybersecurity or cyber resiliency strategies. Using a behavioral-based threat management/threat intelligence model may allow the threat intelligence team to truly think like an attacker. Behavioral-based threat intelligence asks the following questions about adversary behaviors:

- Which are most common?
- Which have the most adverse impacts?
- Which have data readily available?
- Which are most likely to indicate malicious acts?
- Where are the "crown jewels" in the network?

It is also important to remember that threat monitoring should not be conducted in a vacuum and does not end at the perimeter of the network. Relaying threat intelligence information to an internal network monitoring division should be mandatory, as this allows the internal network to understand what type of threat signatures to look for. This allows the organization to continue scanning and monitoring for a specific threat, even if the threat is able to breach the external defenses of the network perimeter. This is crucial, as any steps taken to mitigate the impact of the network breach can protect vital resources of the organization.

4.1.4.4 Reporting on Threat Intelligence

Threat intelligence reports should be timely, fruitful, action oriented, and mindful of the organization's defenses. Threat intelligence reports must be current to allow decision makers and security professionals the opportunity to respond and, if possible, select the correct response for the organization. Threat intelligence reports must be inherently knowledgeable of the organization's defenses in order to determine if the threat is mitigated by current defenses or not. In this manner, it can be determined if the threat truly requires a response that needs additional resources focused on the mitigation. It is at this stage that this threat intelligence becomes a vulnerability management issue. In addition, member organizations that share threat intelligence collectively may require your organization to share any threat intelligence information externally with the larger community. In this case, it is important to cleanse the reporting to ensure that no organizational secrets or exposures remain, but it is equally important to make sure the threat report is still of value to the other members of the community. By keeping important details about the threats within the reports, it allows the information sharing groups to turn the threat data into actionable intelligence. In the context of a strategy, establishing a new threat intelligence unit, or maximizing the potential of an existing threat intelligence unit would be worthwhile initiatives.

Figure 4.4 shows how an organization, once it understands the business environment that it operates in, can develop their own listing of their "top ten threats." The next chapter will show how these threats can then be mapped to critical security controls so that risk management professionals can make a better decision about coverage. This list is a sample of top ten threats – remember that any organization's listing will be different.

As far as the actual contents of the threat reports, the reports should contain the outputs of the threat management methodology. While it is a challenge to develop meaningful metrics from threat monitoring activities, generalizations, and trends can be easily developed and reused.

4.1.4.4.1 Relating Threat Intelligence to the Board

If an organization's current cyber program is on the lower end of the maturity spectrum, chances are the Board has not seen any reporting on threats or threat intelligence during regular reporting sessions. In order to provide the Board with valuable information during the reporting process, care must be taken not to err on the side of unnecessary caution by attempting to scare the Board members. Most Board members do not have a technical background and are growing tired of throwing blank checks at their security organizations with very little tangible benefits to show for it. Remember that one of the most important reasons to develop a strategy for

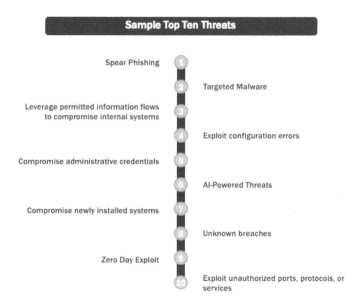

FIGURE 4.4   Sample Top Ten Threats.

cybersecurity or cyber resilience is to understand where the organization's next dollar is best spent. In order to move beyond the scare tactic, it is very crucial to explain the processes of the organization's threat intelligence, the outputs of the process, and how this information is an input into the cyber program and any associated cyber strategies. It is also particularly useful to explain the benefits to tailoring a cyber risk management program – perhaps even an operational risk management program – to the relevant threats an organization faces, not just cyber threats. It is in this arena that a cybersecurity or cyber resilience strategy will shine. By showing Board members meaningful trends of threat intelligence reports, how the strategy uses the quality of these threats and their likelihood of attack as inputs into the strategy, Board members may gain comfort that their cyber programs are trending in the right direction. Or, on the opposite side of the spectrum, by showing Board members the true cyber threat landscape and the likelihood of this threat landscape causing material issues to the organization, the board may decide to allocate more resources to the cyber program. Showing the Board a clear picture of the cybersecurity and cyber resilience programs and the threats each program faces is key to gaining acceptance and credibility for the respective strategies and allows the strategies to succeed. This in turn will allow the board to appreciate that all cyber resources are well utilized.

4.2   VULNERABILITIES

A vulnerability is a cybersecurity term that refers to a flaw in a system that can leave it open to attack. A vulnerability may also refer to any type of weakness in a computer system itself, in the information system, system security procedure, internal control,

TABLE 4.3

Vulnerability Categories and Definitions/Examples

1. Buffer Overflows

   Example: An attacker sends data to a program, which it stores in an undersized stack buffer. The result is that information on the call stack is overwritten, including the function's return pointer. The data sets the value of the return pointer so that when the function returns, it transfers control to malicious code contained in the attacker's data.

2. Unvalidated Input

   Example: Attacker tampers with any part of an HTTP request, including the URL, query string, headers, cookies, form fields, and hidden fields, to try to bypass the sites security mechanisms.

3. Race Conditions

   Definition: A flaw that produces an unexpected result when the timing of actions impacts other actions.

   Example: When the timing of actions impacts other actions, events may happen out of sequence, resulting in anomalous behavior.

4. Access Control Issues

   Definition: Access control governs decisions and processes of determining, documenting, and managing the subjects (users, devices, or processes) that should be granted access and the objects to which they should be granted access; essentially, what is allowed.

5. Weakness in Authentication, Authorization, or Cryptographic Practices

   Example: Passwords that can be brute forced (passwords that can be guessed using random word generators and tried repeatedly), encryption standards that have been proven unreliable.

or process, or in anything that leaves information exposed to a threat. Vulnerabilities are the weaknesses within IT systems and IT processes that serve as the entry points for threat actors to conduct their harm. Table 4.3 outlines the main categories of vulnerabilities with their definitions and examples.

4.2.1 OPEN WEB APPLICATION SECURITY PROJECT (OWASP) APPLICATION SECURITY VULNERABILITIES

Open Web Application Security Project (OWASP) is a not-for-profit open community dedicated to enabling organizations to conceive, develop, acquire, operate, and maintain applications that can be trusted. All of the OWASP tools, documents, forums, and chapters are free and open to anyone interested in improving application security. OWASP advocates approaching application security as a people, process, and technology problem because the most effective approaches to application security include improvements in all of these areas. The following list is a current OWASP Top Ten Cheat Sheet of application security vulnerability types. This list changes from year to year.

1. SQL injection
2. LDAP injection
3. ORM injection
4. ZML injection

5. SSI injection
6. XPath injection
7. IMAP/SMTP injection
8. Cross-site scripting and forgery
9. OS command injection
10. Buffer overflow

4.2.2 IDENTIFYING VULNERABILITIES

Vulnerabilities can be identified and discovered by a number of methods. There are lists of common vulnerabilities that are available online and produced by vendors and security organizations. A good place to start is with one of those lists. Vulnerabilities specific to your organization can be identified by discussions with Information Technology and Audit areas in addition to self-discovery. There exist a myriad of tools and techniques available to identify vulnerabilities. The most commonly used are:

- Vulnerability scanners
- Penetration and/or Red Team testing
- An audit of the organization's operational and management controls

Whatever risk management methodology is used by the organization, there will be an assessment phase that will identify gaps and vulnerabilities. Having a best in class cybersecurity and cyber resiliency program is a game of absolutes. In order to have effective vulnerability and patch management, there must also be effective asset management. As many assets as possible must be known, inventoried, and effectively scanned by a vulnerability scanner in order to facilitate knowledge and awareness of vulnerabilities within the environment. This is important as by performing more in-depth vulnerability scanning, the ability to reduce risk may increase.

Reporting on vulnerability scanning is paramount in the context of a strategy. For example, a report to executives may show a percentage of all assets inventoried that are scanned by the vulnerability scanner. This allows executives to understand that there is an unknown aspect to their environment that could be vulnerable. Reporting to executives, as will be addressed in later chapters, can also be used to tell a story about the vulnerabilities within the environment (e.g., % of vulnerabilities patched, % weekly change of unpatched vulnerabilities). These are some examples of indicators that can be used to quickly give executives a picture of the complete risk posture of the organization.

4.2.2.1 Modern-Day Vulnerability Management Issues

In the modern age, many organizations believe that by installing a vulnerability scanner within their environment and then installing agents of the vulnerability scanners on their key systems they will be protected by all the ills of cyber space. Unfortunately, this is not the case. Some major, but common, weaknesses within cybersecurity and cyber resiliency of organizations are outlined in Table 4.4.

TABLE 4.4

Vulnerability Management Shortfalls

1. Modern security approaches have trouble detecting an advanced persistent threat (APT).
2. Custom scripts developed by well-trained and well-funded hackers are often not detected.
3. Custom hacking tools are often tested against industry standard monitoring and alerting devices.
4. Well-trained and well-funded hackers often use obfuscation technologies or sidetrack attacks to evade malware detection programs and processes.
5. Legitimate functionality within compromised systems often goes undetected.
6. Sufficient data about APT in order to do proper vulnerability analysis is often unavailable.
7. Zero-day vulnerabilities may be known by hacking groups prior to being known by vendors.

4.2.3 ASSET-RELATED VULNERABILITIES

Threats cannot impact assets unless the assets are vulnerable to the specific threats. In addition, mitigating controls may be in place, reducing the likelihood of a threat exploiting a given asset. Understanding the types of vulnerabilities that exist on critical assets is a key step in risk assessment. Comprehensive information security programs require that every asset should have protective measures in the areas of:

- Prevention
- Detection
- Response

Having said so, however, this does not limit controls to these areas within the NIST CSF framework. In fact, the most mature organizations will have invested in controls that suit their needs explicitly and according to the target state they wish to obtain.

Preventative measures reduce the likelihood of exploitation. The ability to detect and respond to incidents allows an organization to minimize losses in the event of exploitation. Furthermore, effective detection and response provide a deterrent to exploitation attempts as well. For each critical asset, the effectiveness of mitigating controls in place will need to be determined. Typical areas of an organization's IT infrastructure to be assessed in terms of the status of mitigating controls might be:

Prevention
- Cybersecurity policies, standards, and procedures
- Current and comprehensive network and application architectures
- Up-to-date software versions and patch levels
- Use of network segmentation and access controls
- Strong authentication/authorization mechanisms
- Enterprise security awareness programs

Detection
- Cyberattack detection capabilities such as logging, associated monitoring, and alerting
- General network intrusion detection capabilities

- Host intrusion detection capabilities
- Incident reporting policy and processes

Response
- Cyber resiliency recovery plan
- Incident response plans and program capabilities
- Response policies and processes
- System back-up and recovery capabilities

4.2.4   COMMON VULNERABILITY SCORING SYSTEM (CVSS)

The Common Vulnerability Scoring System (CVSS) is a free and open industry standard for assessing the severity of computer system security vulnerabilities. CVSS
attempts to assign severity scores to vulnerabilities, allowing responders to prioritize
responses and resources according to threat.

Vulnerabilities that affect critical assets are discovered through interviews, documentation review, and technical analysis. Vulnerabilities are classified based on their
severity. Severity identifies the exposure of an asset:

- Critical – an aspect of a critical requirement which is deficient or vulnerable
  to direct or indirect attack that will create decisive or significant effects
- High – a vulnerability which allows a threat to control/destroy an asset
- Medium – a vulnerability which allows a threat to compromise/access an asset
- Low – a vulnerability which provides threat information which could be
  used to compromise an asset

For each critical asset identified during the asset identification phase, identified vulnerabilities should be noted and classified as shown in Table 4.5. It should be noted
that vulnerability management should be carried out on a regular basis, not just during the initial phases.

As for patching, one of the most important aspects that is not clear in the above table
is that the higher the severity rating – the timelier the organization must be with implementing a patch for the vulnerability. For example, many organizations strive to have
no more than a seven-day window for critical vulnerabilities to be patched – inclusive

---

TABLE 4.5
CVSS v3.0 Vulnerability Severity Ratings

Severity	Base Score Range
None	0.0
Low	0.1–3.9
Medium	4.0–6.9
High	7.0–8.9
Critical	9.0–10.0

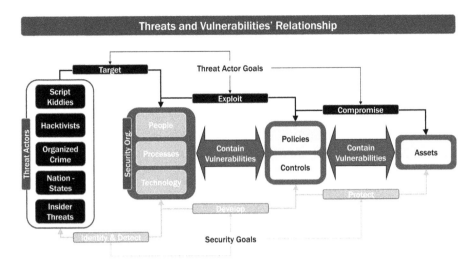

FIGURE 4.5   Adding Vulnerabilities to the Threat Actor Model.

of the reboot required to ensure that the patch is applied correctly. This may or may not be enough time. The more accurate a vulnerability assessment, the more accurate the subsequent risk assessment. The assets and threats that support and impact business operations tend to change much less frequently than the vulnerability analysis. New vulnerabilities, changes in technology, and user/administrator introduced issues all contribute to a dynamic vulnerability environment. Areas identified through this high-level vulnerability assessment are candidates for a detailed, technical assessment.

It is important to understand early on in the cybersecurity and cyber resilience strategy development process that no organization, no matter their operating environment, processes, or controls, is 100% safe from any adverse impacts to confidentiality, integrity, or availability. This means that every organization has vulnerabilities at some points within their business processes – known or unknown. It is up to the cybersecurity and cyber resilience professionals to understand the organization's business processes and the interconnections of technology within those processes. Figure 4.5 shows that security policies, controls, and assets may inherently, or by design, contain vulnerabilities.

Figure 4.5 shows that the very assets the attackers are targeting are indeed protected by policies and controls that may themselves contain exploitable vulnerabilities.

4.2.5   Vulnerabilities in the Context of a Strategy

It should not be any surprise that the main goal of vulnerability management is threefold:

1. Discover vulnerabilities as quick as possible
2. Understand compensating controls, if any, to mitigate the exposure
3. Patch the vulnerability within the shortest amount of time

However, in the context of a strategy, identifying and fixing vulnerabilities is more complex. Vulnerability management is about understanding how different severity levels of different vulnerabilities on specific business processes require tailored attention and varying levels of resources. Successful vulnerability management requires both the correct tools and a well-executed and repeatable process. A strategy should then use the outputs of the vulnerability management process as input to the strategy in order to address further risk reduction. The same goes for the results of the threat management process.

4.3   CYBERATTACKS

A "cybersecurity incident" is "[a]n occurrence that actually or potentially results in adverse consequences to … an information system or the information that the system processes, stores, or transmits and that may require a response action to mitigate the consequences." – as quoted by the U.S. Computer Emergency Readiness Team at niccs.us-cert.gov.

4.3.1   COMMON TYPES OF CYBERATTACKS

There are many types of cyberattacks that can have an adverse impact on an organization's operations. The following list defines and explains some of the most common forms of attacks.

- Malware – a term used to describe any malicious software, including spyware, ransomware, Trojan horses, viruses, worms, and rootkits. It is specifically designed to disrupt, damage, or gain unauthorized access.
  Once inside a system, malware can do the following:
  - Block access to key components of the network and potentially request ransom to unlock it (Ransomware)
  - Disrupt certain components and cause the system to be inoperable
  - Install additional malware or other harmful software
  - Covertly obtain information by transmitting data from the hard drive
- Ransomware – a type of malware attack, has been a focus of executives due to several high-profile attacks. Once ransomware is into a corporate environment, it spreads from machine to machine corrupting files and encrypting the contents of hard drives, thereby rendering the devices useless – a concept known as "bricking" the device. The interesting aspect about ransomware, as the name implies, is the opportunity for the perpetrators to pay a ransom. This trait also separates ransomware from general malware. Usually, the groups behind the attack will have some sort of message that displays on the bricked devices asking for a large sum of a cryptocurrency be transferred to the hackers' cryptocurrency wallet. While this may seem to be an easy way out, success of actually getting encrypted files back and restarting business processes as normal are mixed at best. Some organizations that have paid the ransom to the attackers did not get their files back; some organizations have successfully restarted operations after paying the ransom.

- Phishing – the practice of sending fraudulent communications that appear to come from a reputable source, usually through email. The attacker can also replicate a commonly used website, such as a bank or other service provider. The objective is to capture the user's personal information such as passwords, credit card numbers, etc. This type of attack is widely used, and the fake websites are quite real looking. In some cases, the user will be prompted to enter in his/her password a second time, allowing the attacker to then be able to capture it.
- Man-in-the-Middle (MitM) attacks – These are also known as eavesdropping or hijacking. In this case, the attackers insert themselves into a two-party transaction or communication. Once the attackers interrupt the traffic without detection, they can steal and alter the communication, relaying bogus information.
- Denial-of-Service (DoS) attack – In a DoS attack, the attacker usually sends excessive messages asking the network or server to authenticate requests that have invalid return addresses. In this manner, the attackers attempt to prevent legitimate users from accessing the service.
- Structured Query Language (SQL) injection – A SQL injection occurs when an attacker inserts malicious code into a server that uses SQL and forces the server to reveal information it normally would not by inserting nefarious SQL statements into an entry field for execution.
- Zero-Day exploit – A zero-day exploit hits after a network vulnerability is announced but before a patch or solution is implemented by the developer or vendor. Attackers target the disclosed vulnerability during this short window of time. It is called a zero-day exploit as the developers have zero days and zero time to fix the bug.

4.3.2   Typical Types of Losses Due to Cyberattacks

If proper threat management and vulnerability management are not conducted, the list below describes some of the likely outcomes that could occur. The following list is general in nature and captures the types of losses an organization might face due to a cyberattack at a high level.

1. Loss of revenue directly related to system downtime of income producing or transaction processing systems. Commonly known as a "Business Interruption" loss
2. Loss of strategic information that can affect the competitive standing of the company and loss of market share
3. Reputational damage that can affect customer and/or investor confidence, potentially lowering company stock prices
4. Forensics costs of discovery of the breach with countermeasures and controls to stop and prevent further damage
5. Data recovery costs from potential going to a full or partial failover site, then returning online to the main site
6. Loss of Intellectual Property (IP) that can be used by the competition in the future

7. Cybersecurity enhancements costs that augment cybersecurity prevention and detection tools and techniques, additional security training, and security procedure development
8. Outright loss of data and equipment that can or cannot be replaced from backup. Commonly known as "Bricking"
9. Increased public relations cost in order to inform the necessary parties of the breach
10. Possible court settlements and fees due to future litigations and possible regulatory penalties cost from state and federal governmental authorities and non-US authorities
11. Breach notifications cost to comply with notifications requirements
12. Increased customer protection costs that may require upgrading customer software/hardware at the home site or customer site
13. Increased insurance premiums for cyber insurance going forward

NOTES

1. MITRE ATT&CK: Design and Philosophy, July 2018 (ATT&CK Use Cases, Section 3 Page 5)
2. MITRE ATT&CK: Design and Philosophy, July 2018 (ATT&CK Use Cases, Section 1, Page 1)
3. MITRE ATT&CK: Design and Philosophy, July 2018 (ATT&CK Use Cases, Section 2, Page 3)

5 Cyber Risks and Controls

5.1 CYBER RISK

Cyber risk can be defined as risk of financial loss and/or disruption or damage to the reputation of an organization from a failure of its information technology systems. There are a number of frameworks and evaluation methods for determining cyber risk. One or more may have already been selected and approved by the organization. If not, it is important that one be chosen and ratified for use in the risk evaluation and performance measurement process. Selecting the enterprise-wide risk assessment process will facilitate results acceptance by the governing bodies.

5.1.1 CYBER RISK FRAMEWORK

Figure 5.1 shows a graphical representation of Threats, Vulnerabilities, Risk Categories, and Controls. This Framework incorporates the threats and vulnerabilities from Chapter 4, but now adds the cyber risk piece.

An assessment of the risks facing the organization must be performed to accurately determine the nature and severity of the risks. The organization's top vulnerabilities must be determined as well. Ultimately, the controls that are put into place must compensate and mitigate these risks, staying within the risk tolerance level of the organization. By enabling a risk-based approach, organizations are addressing the most pressing and costly threats.

5.1.2 RISK CATEGORY DEFINITIONS

According to the National Institute of Standards and Technology (NIST), risk is defined as a measure of the extent to which an entity is threatened by a potential circumstance or event and is typically a function of: (i) the adverse impacts that would arise if the circumstance or event occurs, and (ii) the likelihood of occurrence.

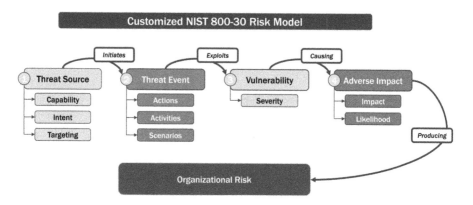

FIGURE 5.1   Customized NIST 800 Risk Model.

However, there are many ways to categorize risk. From an organizational view, business risk can be broken down into many components. All are relevant with respect to cybersecurity and cyber resiliency. The following typical business risks should be considered when constructing an enterprise-wide cyber risk profile and evaluation approach:

- Security and Resiliency Risk – any event that could result in the compromise of organizational assets, i.e., the unauthorized use, loss, damage, disclosure or modification of organizational assets for the profit, personal interest or political interests of individuals, groups or other entities.
- Information Technology Risk – missed opportunities to use technology to improve efficiency or effectiveness of existing business processes, or as an enabler for new business initiatives[1].
- Operational Risk – the risk not inherent in financial, systematic, or market-wide risk. It is the risk remaining after determining financing and systematic risk, and includes risks resulting from breakdowns in internal procedures, people, and systems. Operational risk can include security and resiliency risk.
- Reputational Risk – a threat or danger to the good name or standing of a business or entity. This risk is hard to quantify but is of the utmost importance to any organization.
- Compliance Risk – exposure to legal penalties, financial forfeiture, and material loss an organization faces when it fails to act in accordance with industry laws and regulations, internal policies, or prescribed best practices.
- Legal Risk – the risk of financial or reputational loss that can result from lack of awareness or misunderstanding of, ambiguity in, or reckless indifference to, the way law and regulation apply to the business, its relationships, processes, products, and services.
- Program Risk – the potential outcome that causes a program to fail to meet its goals. Program risk is not just the sum of the risk of the individual

projects in that program, but needs to take into account any uncertain event that may affect one of the following:

- Scope
- Schedule
- Cost
- Quality
- Performance

Additional factors such as an organization's project management procedures, certain external influences, and any relevant regulatory constraints may also play a role in overall program risk.

- Strategic Risk – can be defined as the risk associated with future plans and strategies, including plans for entering new services, expanding existing services through enhancements (e.g., enhancing infrastructure).

    Strategic risk can also be defined as current and prospective impact of strategic decisions made by management arising from adverse business decisions, improper implementation of decisions, or lack of responsiveness to industry changes. In order to best construct strategic objectives, organizations should follow the industry standard of a "SMART" guideline, where a strategic objective should be:

- Specific
- Measurable
- Appropriate
- Realistic
- Timely

To do so will utilize a common measurement approach to objectives that can later be analyzed and evaluated.

5.1.3   RISK TOLERANCE AND RISK APPETITE

Risk tolerance and risk appetite are closely connected and should be determined at the enterprise level. When the risk measurement methodology is selected, the degree of risk that will be acceptable should reside in accordance with these predetermined boundaries.

5.1.3.1   Risk Appetite

Risk appetite, as defined by the Committee of Sponsoring Organizations of the Treadway Commission (COSO), is the broad-based amount of risk a company or other entity is willing to accept in pursuit of its mission or vision. Cyber risk appetite can be defined as the aggregate level of cyber risk an organization is willing to accept, or to avoid, in order to achieve its business objectives.

When considering the risk appetite levels for an enterprise, two major factors are important:

1. The enterprise's objective capacity to absorb loss; e.g., financial loss, reputation damage, etc., in other words, the acceptable level of risk exposure.
2. The culture of the organization toward risk taking – cautious or aggressive: the amount of loss the enterprise is willing to accept.

There is no standard for quantifying risk appetite. It can and will be different for different companies. Risk appetite is an important concept and should be qualified and quantified (if possible) by senior management for the organization as a whole. Individual business units should be in unison with the designated enterprise levels.

5.1.3.2 Risk Tolerance

While risk appetite sets the levels of risk the organization is willing to take, risk tolerance sets reality limits on what can be dealt with. Risk tolerance is defined as the boundaries of risk taking outside of which the organization is not prepared to venture in the pursuit of its long-term objectives. Risk tolerance measures the organization's level of risk adverseness.

5.1.3.3 Risk Appetite vs. Risk Tolerance

Figure 5.2 shows a representation of the risk continuum. The section on the far left is where the risk is the lowest. The section in the middle is the designated organizational risk appetite allowance. The two sections to the right of the middle one indicate the risk tolerance levels where the risk is highest. It is up to the organization to quantify these areas according to their risk management policies.

Risk appetite and risk tolerance can change over time due to factors such as changes in technology, new business strategies, or shifts in corporate culture.

5.1.4 CYBER RISK MEASUREMENT METHODOLOGIES

Cyber risk is a pervasive issue. There are a number of methods available today to qualify and quantify cyber risk. This section will present a sample of methods for addressing cybersecurity and cyber resiliency risk. Some provide qualification of risk, some quantification, some both. Some are simple, some can involve complex formulas and might involve statistical methods such as Monte Carlo simulations which can be used for advanced calculations. In all cases, risk must be assessed, and cybersecurity and cyber resiliency strategies must be created with objectives and corresponding initiatives that mitigate the cyber risk to the organization's acceptable levels.

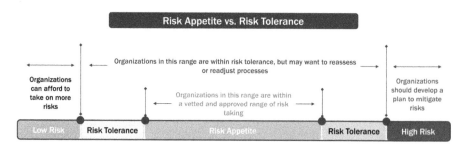

FIGURE 5.2   Risk Appetite vs. Risk Tolerance.

Before performing a risk assessment, some basic questions need to be answered. These five questions apply to all the methodologies discussed below. They are:

1. What are the threat sources?
2. What are the threat events?
3. What are the vulnerabilities?
4. What is the likelihood that the vulnerabilities can be exploited?
5. What is the potential impact of the cyberattack?

After answering these questions, any of the cyber risk measurement methodologies mentioned below can be used. The NIST Special Publications (SP) 800-30, however, provides a practical methodology for measuring cyber risk.

5.1.4.1   US National Institute of Standards and Technology's Special Publications 800-30

NIST has developed a risk assessment process as shown in Figure 5.3 that takes all these factors into consideration.

NIST Special Publication 800-30 Revision 1 (September 2012) is a Guide for Conducting Risk Assessments. Special Publications (SPs) are developed and issued by NIST as recommendations and guidance documents. Federal agencies

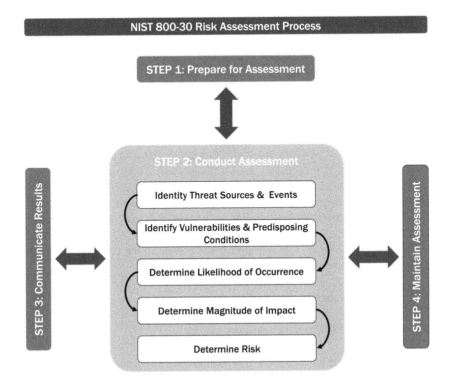

FIGURE 5.3   NIST 800-30 Risk Assessment Process.

(not National security programs) must follow the NIST SP as mandated in a Federal Information Processing Standard (FIPS 200). The Special Publication gives detailed guidance about what needs to be considered when evaluating likelihood and impact of threats and vulnerabilities resulting in an overall risk calculation. The Special Publication has a number of tables and charts of types of impacts, threat sources, likelihood of threat events, and levels of risk (combination of likelihood and impact) that provide a comprehensive methodology for evaluating risk. The Special Publication identifies five types of threats that nearly every organization faces:

1. *Unauthorized access* – This can be both adversarial and nonadversarial in nature, potentially occurring from an attack, malware or even just employee error.
2. *Misuse of information by authorized users* – This is typically an insider threat that can occur when data is altered, deleted, or used without approval.
3. *Data leaks/accidental exposure of PII* – Personal Identifying Information (PII) is considered breached anytime it is altered, deleted, or disclosed to an unauthorized party.
4. *Loss of data* – It occurs when an organization loses or accidentally deletes data as a result of a botched backup or poor replication.
5. *Service/productivity disruptions* – It occurs when services and operations are interrupted.

The question always remaining is how to apply these methodologies in a real-world manner, with real numbers and numeric results. Below is one interpretation of how to perform a cyber risk assessment using the NIST 800-30 standard.

5.1.5   A NIST 800-30 CYBER RISK ASSESSMENT EXAMPLE

A modified cyber risk assessment methodology is presented so that it can be used as a more practical application of the standard. This methodology can be used as a measure of performance of the strategy. A risk assessment can be done when the Strategy is invoked, and then again after one year (or at any point in time). The reduction in risk (mitigation of the risk) will attest to the validity of the strategy.

Organizations can modify or interpret the variables of the calculation shown in Table 5.1. In this example, the variables are:

1. The assets and their assigned values
2. The threats and their respective ratings
3. The vulnerabilities and their severity ratings

Scales of 1–5 are used for Impact Magnitude and Asset Value calculations, while the Threat Rating scale is 1–10. These scales can be changed to better reflect

TABLE 5.1

NIST Risk Descriptions for Government Entities

Qualitative Values	Description
Very High	Very high risk means that a threat event could be expected to have multiple severe or catastrophic adverse effects on organizational operations, organizational assets, individuals, other organizations, or the Nation.
High	High risk means that a threat event could be expected to have a severe or catastrophic adverse effect on organizational operations, organizational assets, individuals, other organizations, or the Nation.
Moderate	Moderate risk means that a threat event could be expected to have a serious effect on organizational operations, organizational assets, individuals, other organizations, or the Nation.
Low	Low risk means that a threat event could be expected to have a limited effect on organizational operations, organizational assets, individuals, other organizations, or the Nation.
Very Low	Very low risk means that a threat event could be expected to have a negligible effect on organizational operations, organizational assets, individuals, other organizations, or the Nation.

the organization's rating methods, if so desired. Figure 5.4 presents the actual formula used in the calculation of the total risk score per asset in Figure 5.5 shown directly after.

Determining the risk calculation of an asset is critical in determining the overall risk of a project or initiative. Projects and initiatives engage assets. In this manner, the overall risk of a project can be projected by examining the risk of its components.

Presented in Figure 5.5 is a simplification of the NIST 800-30 Rev 1 formula, where the total Risk Score per Asset is calculated. Here the total risk score of many assets are calculated and then scaled relative to each other.

Below is a walk-through of how the spreadsheet depicted in Figure 5.5 was created. The following steps should be taken in order to create this type of table while performing a cyber assessment:

1. *ASSETS*
   a. Identify the assets of importance (high value) including people, processes, and technology. These are the assets that will be affected and/or involved in the cyber initiatives
   b. Identify some assets of lesser value in order to see the comparative difference in the final Risk Rating result
   c. List assets in Column B
   d. Rate the asset values

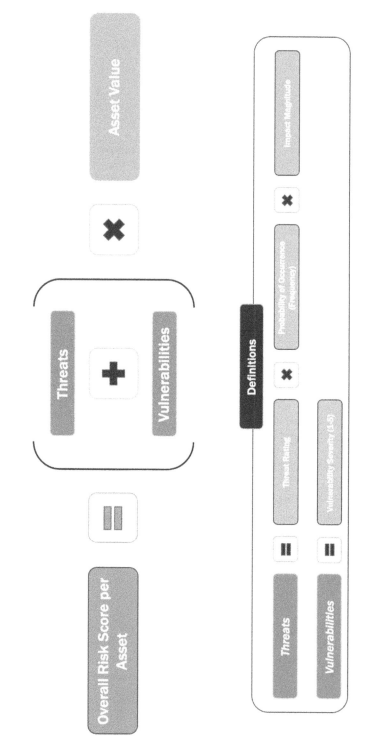

FIGURE 5.4   Cyber Risk Score per Asset Formula.

CUSTOMIZED NIST 800-30 CYBER RISK ASSESSMENT EXAMPLE

		THREATS					VULNERABILITIES Vulnerability Severity (1 = Low, 5 = Critical)					TOTAL RISK SCORE (Sum of Cell Values for Assets)	RISK RATING RESULT
		Unauthorized Use / Access - Account Compromised	Misuse of information by Authorized Users	Data leaks/ PII Exposure	Loss of Data	Service/ Productivity Disruptions	Sensitive Data Exposure	Data Theft	Injection	Failure to System Patch	Security Mis-Configuration	L = 110 or less M = 111-190 H = over 190	High, Medium, Low
Threat Rating (1-Low, 10 = High)		4	5	8	9	10	5	4	3	3	3		
Probability of Occurance (%)		25%	25%	50%	15%	2%							
Impact Magnitude (1 = Negligable, 5 = High)		5	4	5	3	5							
ASSETS: People, Processes, Technology	**Asset Value (1-5)**												
Human Resources Data - People and Organization	3	15	15	60	12	3	15	12	9	9	9	159	M
Network Infrastructure	4.5	23	23	23	23	23	23	18	14	14	14	194	H
Project Management Processes	2.5	13	13	13	13	13	13	10	8	8	8	108	L
Financial - Data Repositories	4.5	23	23	23	23	23	23	18	14	14	14	194	H
E-Commerce - Information Systems	2.5	13	13	13	13	13	13	10	8	8	8	108	L
System Life Cycle Environments	3.5	18	18	18	18	18	18	14	11	11	11	151	M
Cyber Policies, Standards and Procedures	3	15	15	15	15	15	15	12	9	9	9	129	M
Financial Applications	4.5	23	23	23	23	23	23	18	14	14	14	194	H
External/InternetCommunications Links	4.5	23	23	23	23	23	23	18	14	14	14	194	H
Data Center IT Infrastructure	4.5	23	23	23	23	23	23	18	14	14	14	194	H
BU Self-Assessment Processes	2.5	13	13	13	13	13	13	10	8	8	8	108	L
Cybersecurity Software	5	25	25	25	25	25	25	20	15	15	15	215	H

FIGURE 5.5 Customized NIST 800-30 Cyber Risk Assessment Example.

2. *THREATS*
   a. Identify a number of top threats facing the organization
   b. List the Threats across Row 7 in columns
   c. Review the Center for Internet Security (CIS) Top 20 Controls as examples
   d. Set the Rating Scales for the threats
       i.   Threat Rating (1-10)
       ii. Probability of occurrence of each threat (x%)
       iii. Impact magnitude of each threat (1-5)
   e. Rate each threat (1-10)
   f. Assign a % probability of occurrence to each threat
   g. Assign an impact magnitude for each threat
3. *THREAT CALCULATIONS*
   a. For each threat, multiply:

The Threat Rating $\times$ Probability of Occurrence $\times$ Impact Magnitude $\times$ Asset Value

   b. This result is value of the threat for this asset. In the case of the first asset – Human Resource Data, the formula becomes: $4 \times 25\% \times 5 \times 3 = 15$
   c. The value 15 goes in the first column under the Unauthorized Use threat and to the right of the first asset – Human Resource Data
   d. Continue across the spreadsheet for each threat for Human Resource Data
   e. Then proceed down the list of assets and perform the same multiplication filling in all the boxes under Threats
4. *VULNERABILITIES*
   a. In the Vulnerabilities section of the spreadsheet, list the most important Vulnerability types and their corresponding severity rating (1–5)
   b. The values opposite each asset in the vulnerabilities section then become:
       i.   The Asset value $\times$ the Vulnerability type's Rating
       ii. In the case of Human Resource Data, this formula becomes $3 \times 5 = 15$
   c. Fill in the remainder of the Vulnerability ratings for each asset
5. *TOTAL RISK SCORE*
   a. To arrive at the Total Risk Score per asset, sum the numbers across the spreadsheet for each asset (include the numbers for both the threats and the vulnerabilities). In the case of Human Resource Data, this sum becomes 159
6. *RISK RATING RESULT*
   a. Derive a scale from the resultant numbers, differentiating them into buckets of High, Medium, and Low (HML) (or any other type of rating desired – see Table 5.2).
   b. Classify all the assets High, Medium, or Low (HML) according to their scores.

TABLE 5.2

NIST Adversarial Threat Ratings

Qualitative Values	Description
Very High	The adversary has a very sophisticated level of expertise, is well resourced, and can generate opportunities to support multiple successful, continuous, and coordinated attacks.
High	The adversary has a sophisticated level of expertise, with significant resources and opportunities to support multiple successful coordinated attacks.
Moderate	The adversary has moderate resources, expertise, and opportunities to support multiple successful attacks.
Low	The adversary has limited resources, expertise, and opportunities to support a successful attack.
Very Low	The adversary has very limited resources, expertise, and opportunities to support a successful attack.

    c. After all assets have been risk assessed using this methodology:
       i. The assets can be addressed in terms of controls
      ii. The risk rating can be performed as a point in time; i.e., at the beginning of the year, at the end of the year, or by quarter
     iii. By performing at multiple time intervals, a risk mitigation trend can be graphed
    d. This method can be used as a measure of performance of the Strategy. An example of this trend is shown in Chapter 7 in Figure 7.6 Cybersecurity and Cyber Resiliency Yearly Report, which charts the Business Unit Quarterly Risk Mitigation for 3 sample Business Units

NOTE: What is important to remember here is that all or some of the assets: People, Processes, and Technology will be utilized when operationalizing the individual cyber initiatives.

5.1.5.1 NIST Risk Descriptions for Government Entities

NIST offers more complete descriptions for evaluating and presenting total risk scores. They are listed in Table 5.1.

5.1.5.2 NIST Adversarial Threat Ratings

NIST further defines its risk ratings levels as shown in Table 5.2. These can be used in lieu or in conjunction with a threat rating scale of 1–10.

5.1.6 OTHER WELL-KNOWN CYBER RISK ASSESSMENT METHODOLOGIES

There exist a number of other standard risk methodologies that can be used by large or small companies without engaging mathematicians or statisticians.

It will be up to the organization to select the method and/or framework that best measures their cyber risk with respect to their business goals, tempered by their risk tolerance and appetite.

The well-known frameworks are:

1. NIST Special Publication 800-30 Revision 1 (September 2012) is a Guide for Conducting Risk Assessments
2. ISACA Risk Framework – Risk IT[2]
3. The International Organization for Standardization/International Electrotechnical Commission's (ISO/IEC) 27005[3]
4. A Guide to the Project Management Body of Knowledge (PMBOK® Guide)
5. Open Web Application Security Project™ (OWASP)
6. The Committee of sponsoring Organizations of the Treadway Commission (COSO) 2013 Framework
7. Factor Analysis of Information Risk (FAIR)[4]
8. Carnegie Mellon® Risk Quantification Method (CM RQM)[5]

5.1.6.1   ISACA Risk Framework – Risk IT[6]

Risk management is a vast discipline for which there are many interpretations. Risk IT is a set of guiding principles to help organizations identify, govern, and effectively manage IT risk. The framework complements CobiT®, a framework on governance and controls for IT-based solutions and services.

Risk management, as defined by ISACA's "The Risk IT Framework"[7], is the process of identifying vulnerabilities and threats to the information resources used by an organization in achieving business objectives and deciding what countermeasures to take in reducing risk to an acceptable level, based on the value of the information resource to the organization. The ISACA Framework concentrates on:

- Risk governance
- Risk evaluation
- Risk response

As stated by the framework, IT risk is business risk – specifically, the business risk associated with the use, ownership, operation, involvement, influence, and adoption of IT within an enterprise. It consists of IT-related events that could potentially impact the business. And, in fact, IT events can cripple a business. As time goes on, more and more functions are computerized, and IT has become a critical mass in running and preserving on-going business. This is why cyber resiliency has mushroomed in importance. Without strategies to provide continuity of business, companies can lose customers, suppliers, money, their reputation, and all-important data.

5.1.6.2   The International Organization for Standardization/
International Electrotechnical Commission's (ISO/IEC) 27000

ISO, as defined by ISO.ORG, is an organization that publishes international standards. The ISO/IEC 2700 family addresses Information Security Management

Systems (ISMS). This family of standards helps organizations keep information assets such as financial information, intellectual property, employee details, or information entrusted to you by third parties.

Like other ISO management system standards, certification to ISO/IEC 27001 is possible but not obligatory. Implementing the standard is considered a "best practice", getting certified in the standard will reassure customers and clients that its recommendations have been followed. The actual certification process would be done by a third party. Additionally, certification can be a useful tool to add credibility, by demonstrating that your product or service meets the certain industry standard requirements. For some industries, certification is a legal or contractual requirement.

As ISO.ORG explains, the standard doesn't specify, recommend, or even name any specific risk management method. It does however imply a continual process consisting of a structured sequence of activities, some of which are iterative:

- Establish the risk management context;
- Quantitatively or qualitatively assess relevant information risks, taking into account the information assets, threats, existing controls, and vulnerabilities to determine the likelihood of incidents or incident scenarios, and the predicted business consequences if they were to occur, to determine a "level of risk";
- Treat the risks appropriately, using those "levels of risk" to prioritize them;
- Keep stakeholders informed throughout the process; and
- Monitor and review risks, risk treatments, obligations and criteria on an ongoing basis, identifying and responding appropriately to significant changes.

5.1.6.3   A Guide to the Project Management Body of Knowledge (PMBOK® Guide)

The PMBOK® is a set of standard terminology and guidelines for project management. One of its ten project management knowledge areas is Project Risk Management. This knowledge area discusses the plan of how risks will be itemized, categorized, and prioritized. The risk analysis used by this method first identifies the risks, classifies them according to likelihood and impact, and then prioritizes them. This methodology can be extremely useful in evaluating project risk. As each strategic goal is comprised of many individual projects, the success of each project can be measured in order to provide a means of determining overall strategic objective achievement. This is a quantitative method of measuring plan performance.

Details of the PMBOK® project risk management can be found in the Guide; however, it is relevant to note here some of its major characteristics. Probability is defined as the ratio of the number of outcomes in an exhaustive set of equally likely outcomes that produce a given event to the total number of possible outcomes – or more simply stated: the measure of the likelihood that an event will occur. Impact is defined as having a strong effect on someone or something.

MITRE Corporation describes impact, as it relates to risk, as having to do with the assessment of the probabilities and consequences of risk events if they are realized. After the risks are assessed, they can be prioritized, and a risk mitigation plan can be created. Applying this methodology to the strategy, risk mitigation will occur at the initiative implementation phase. Each of the initiatives that comprise a strategic objective will mitigate some portion of the overall cyber risk.

5.1.6.4 Open Web Application Security Project™ (OWASP) Risk Rating Methodology[8]

The OWASP methodology provides guidance and methodologies re-performing security risk analysis. OWASP uses a standard risk model as shown in Figure 5.6.

The OWASP methodology has several steps:

1. Identify a security risk and its likelihood of occurrence
2. Define the threat agent and kind of attack, considering skill level, motive, opportunity, and size of the threat agent group(s)
3. Identify the vulnerability involved considering the ease of discovery, ease of exploit, awareness of the vulnerability, and intrusion detection capabilities
4. Determine the impact of a successful exploit. Impact on the system can be measured in loss of confidentiality, integrity, availability, and accountability. Impact can also be measured in business terms in terms of financial, reputational, noncompliance, and privacy damage.

These ratings are based on a scale of 0–9, as shown in Figure 5.7.

The estimation of Likelihood is a mean between different factors in a 0 to 9 scale:

1. Threat agent factors – skill level, motive, opportunity, size
2. Vulnerability factors – ease of discovery, ease of exploit, awareness, intrusion detection

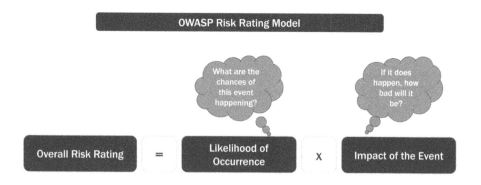

FIGURE 5.6   OWASP Risk Rating Model.

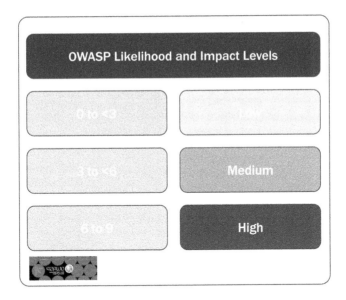

FIGURE 5.7   OWASP Likelihood and Impact Levels.

The estimation of impact as a mean between different factors in a 0 to 9 scale:

1. Technical impact factors – loss of confidentiality, integrity, availability, accountability
2. Business impact factors – the level of business risk justifies investment in the security spend

The next step is to rate the threat agents, the vulnerability factors, the technical impact, and the business impact. The OWASP risk rating methodology is a proven, repeatable model and is widely used. The overall risk severity can be charted as shown in Figure 5.8 as low, medium, high, and critical.

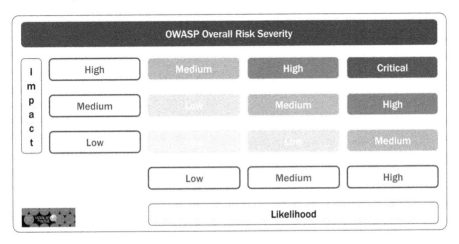

FIGURE 5.8   OWASP Overall Risk Severity.

TABLE 5.3
COSO ERM Framework

1. Control Environment
   - Integrity and Ethical Values
   - Commitment to Competence
   - Board of Directors and Audit Committee
   - Management's Philosophy and Operating Style
   - Organizational Structure
   - Assignment of Authority and Responsibility
   - Human Resource Policies and Procedures
2. Risk Assessment
   - Company-wide Objectives
   - Process-level Objectives
   - Risk Identification and Analysis
   - Managing Change
3. Control Activities
   - Policies and Procedures
   - Security (Application and Network)
   - Application Change Management
   - Business Continuity/Backups
   - Outsourcing
4. Information and Communication
   - Quality of Information
   - Effectiveness of Communication
5. Monitoring
   - Ongoing Monitoring
   - Separate Evaluations
   - Reporting Deficiencies

Other methodologies use different terms for their likelihood and impact and can then be charted in a slightly different manner. In one case, probability can be ranked as not likely, very likely, and critical and impact as negligible, marginal, critical, and catastrophic.

5.1.6.5   Committee of Sponsoring Organization of the Treadway Commission (COSO) Enterprise Risk Management (ERM)[9]

The COSO ERM Framework talks about assessment, planning, coordination, and implementation as the four phases. COSO has five components shown in Table 5.3.

The components work to establish the foundation for the internal control structure of the company through leadership and governance, shared values, and company culture. Many organizations have adopted the COSO framework as it has great value.

5.1.6.6   Factor Analysis of Information Risk (FAIR)[10]

The FAIR methodology can be used by an organization for analyzing, quantifying, and managing risk. The FAIR Institute is a nonprofit professional organization dedicated to advancing the discipline of measuring and managing information risk. The

FAIR methodology is an international standard quantitative model for cyber security and operational risk, which can quantify information risk in financial terms. It provides information risk, cybersecurity standards, and best practices to help organization measure, manage, and report on information risk.

5.1.6.6.1 FAIR Example Goals, Sub Goals, Questions, and Metrics

FAIR provides usable, business-related information security metrics as shown in Table 5.4, which shows a one-to-many relationship between Goals and Metrics.

TABLE 5.4
FAIR Example Goals, Sub Goals, Questions, and Metrics

Goals	Sub Goals	Questions	Metrics
Cost effective	Not over or under control	Are we aligned with risk appetite?	Acceptable level of risk Current risk level
	Optimize solution selection	What is the most cost-effective solution?	Solution costs Solution benefits
	Acceptable rate of progress	Are we progressing toward objectives at the proper rate?	Milestone risks Current risk condition Previous risk condition Elapsed time Forecast risk condition
	Efficient operations	Are we focused on the most important things?	Areas of risk concentration Key control deficiencies
		Is the full cost benefit of our resources being realized?	Resource utilization Resource cost
Achieve	Good risk landscape visibility	Do we have good visibility?	Threat Intelligence Asset management Control conditions Impact factors
	Know the gap	How far away from alignment are we?	Acceptable level of risk Current risk level
	Close the gap	Where does risk exist?	Risk assessments Self-identified points of exposure Loss events
		What control deficiencies exist?	Risk assessments Self-identified deficiencies Loss events
Maintain	Good risk management visibility	Do we have good risk management visibility?	Asset visibility Threat visibility Controls visibility Impact factor visibility Decision visibility Execution visibility
	Remediate cause of variance	Which root causes are driving variance into the environment?	Variance data Root cause analysis results

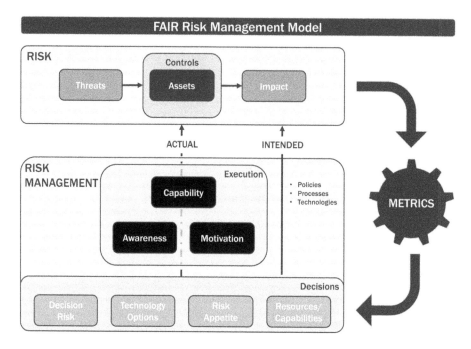

FIGURE 5.9   FAIR Risk Management Model.[11]

Organizations should create their own tailored security metrics relating back to the critical success factors derived from the list in Table 2.2.

5.1.6.6.2 FAIR Risk Management Model

The FAIR methodology proposes a landscape of three elements as shown in Figure 5.9. They are Risk, Risk Management, and Metrics.

The RISK component is comprised of threats, assets, controls, and impact factors. The RISK MANAGEMENT component contains decisions and execution requirements. The decisions that have to be made affect the people, policies, processes, and technologies of the organization. The people responsible for the execution need to have three things:

1. To have the capability (skills and resources) and authority to execute the decisions
2. To have awareness of the expected outcomes and their effect on the organization
3. Be motivated to follow through on the execution of the decisions

The ACTUAL versus the INTENDED is the difference in the amount of RISK that is being managed by the RISK MANAGEMENT component. This is an important concept, as it is highly likely that ACTUAL is less than INTENDED and visually shows the decisions made by the risk management organization must be executed appropriately through capabilities, awareness, and motivation.

The METRICS provide feedback from the results of the risk associated with the threats over the assets and their corresponding controls. This feedback tempers the decisions regarding the management of the risk, thereby creating a continuous loop.

5.1.6.7 Carnegie Mellon® Risk Quantification Method (CM RQM)[5]

The Carnegie Mellon University Software Engineering Institute (SEI) researchers undertook a project funded by the US Department of Defense in 2010, to define what constitutes best practice for risk management. The SEI has conducted research and development in the area of risk management since the early 1990s. The SEI researchers have specified a risk management framework that documents accepted best practice for risk management and an approach for evaluation of a program's or organization's risk management practice in relation to the framework.

The Carnegie Mellon® Risk Quantification Method provides a consistent way to define and evaluate cyber risk scenarios. They are evaluated at two points in time. The first time occurs before any risk mitigation is applied – that is when the risk is purely inherent risk. The inherent risk can be approximated in a qualitative fashion by posing a series of questions regarding the nature of the threat and the threat actor(s). The second analysis occurs after risk mitigation by posing the same set of questions. The threats can be threats to the organization's business, operations, revenues, data integrity, reputation, legal status, etc. The business impact can be ranked (for example) on a scale from 1-5. A risk index is developed at the initial pass through the questions. The second pass at a later date in time shows the projected residual risk: the risk after mitigation. Note that the set of questions can be derived by the company itself or by a third-party contractor.

The Carnegie Mellon® Risk Quantification Method involves the following parameters:

1. Scenario – the description of where, how, etc., the threat will occur
2. Business Impact – relates to the specific scenario described
3. Threat – the threat actor(s) that are appropriate for the business being evaluated
4. Imminence – how timely this threat and scenario are to occur
5. Likelihood – how likely this threat and scenario are to occur
6. Maturity of Controls – this characteristic can be evaluated using the NIST CSF controls method

5.1.6.7.1 Carnegie Mellon® Risk Quantification Method Risk Index

The score ranges for each of the parameters can have different total values, depending on how it is decided to rank them. The risk score is then calculated by the following formula in Figure 5.10.

5.1.7 RISK DISCLOSURE: THE SECURITIES AND EXCHANGE COMMISSION (SEC) GUIDANCE ON RISK (FEB 2018)

In February 2018, the Securities and Exchange Commission (SEC) issued interpretive guidance to assist public companies in preparing disclosures about cybersecurity risks

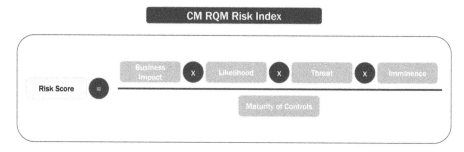

FIGURE 5.10   Carnegie Mellon® Risk Quantification Method Index.

and incidents. The guidance reminds companies that federal securities laws require them to disclose information about material cybersecurity risks and incidents.

Item 503(c) of Regulation S-K and Item 3.D of Form 20-F require companies to disclose the most significant factors that make investments in the company's securities speculative or risky. Companies should disclose the risks associated with cybersecurity and cybersecurity incidents if these risks are among such factors, including risks that arise in connection with acquisitions.

It's advisable for companies to consider the following issues, among others, in evaluating cybersecurity risk factor disclosure:

- A company's protocols relating to or efforts to minimize, cybersecurity risks and its capacity, and any measures taken, to respond to cybersecurity incidents
- Whether a particular cybersecurity incident is likely to occur or recur
- How a company is prioritizing cybersecurity risks, incidents, and defense
- The probability of the occurrence and potential magnitude of cybersecurity incidents
- The aspects of the company's business and operations that give rise to material cybersecurity risks and the potential costs and consequences of such risks, including industry-specific risks and third-party supplier and service provider risks

Although this legislation applies to public companies, it should also be followed by private ones as well, as it sets the minimal requirements for a risk-based approach to a company's cybersecurity and cyber resiliency strategy. The strategy should include a continuous evaluation of threats, vulnerabilities, and their associated risks. The risks should be prioritized, and mitigation efforts be launched in the form of initiatives, projects, and programs and be ongoing in nature.

5.2   IT CONTROLS

Traditionally speaking, there are two classes of controls:

1. *General Controls:* Information Technology (IT) general controls (ITGC) are the basic controls that can be applied to IT systems such as

applications, operating systems, databases, and supporting IT infrastructure. The objectives of general controls are to ensure the confidentiality, integrity, and availability (CIA) of the data, processes, and systems of the organization.

2. *Application Controls:* Application controls are processes and procedures that prevent the application from veering from its intended objective. Application controls can govern input, processing, and output functions ensuring that the data is complete, accurate, and valid.

5.2.1 MAIN FUNCTIONS OF CONTROLS

Controls can also be defined in terms of the functions they perform. The four types of main functions are deterrent, preventative, detective, and corrective are defined below.

- *Deterrent Controls* – are intended to discourage a potential attacker. For example, establishing an information security policy, a warning message on the logon screen, a lock, or security cameras.
- *Preventive Controls* – are intended to minimize the likelihood of an incident occurring. For example, a user account management process, restricting server room access to authorized personnel, configuring appropriate rules on a firewall, or implementing an access control list on a file share.
- *Detective Controls* – are intended to identify when an incident has occurred. For example, review of server or firewall security logs or Intrusion Detection System (IDS) alerts.
- *Corrective Controls* – are intended to fix information system components after an incident has occurred. For example, data backups, SQL transaction log shipping, or business continuity and disaster recovery plans.

However, there are additional types of controls such as predictive and containment as Figure 5.11 shows. Controls can be directed at specific types of incidents (threat, vulnerability, risk, or issue). In general, the objective of controls is prediction, deterrence, detection, mitigation, or containment. In some cases, there exists a one-to-many relationship.

Each organization is encouraged to do a similar mapping of controls to incident type, breaking down further the threats, vulnerabilities, and risks/issues of the organization into subcategories. In this fashion, it can be seen if there exist specific controls per incident sub-type.

5.2.2 MATURITY OF CONTROLS

Once again, the NIST CSF model provides a structure for determining the maturity of controls: the top-level capabilities of Identify, Protect, Detect, Respond, and Recover are further broken down into more specific controls. The projects and/or initiatives that are set in motion to address the gaps identified within these capabilities

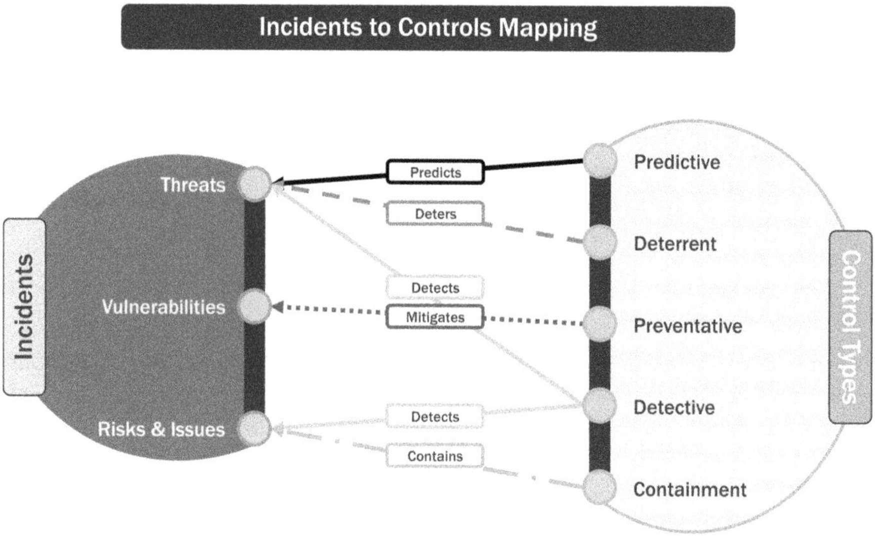

FIGURE 5.11   Incidents to Controls Mapping.

after the various assessments are in fact, the "controls". Over time, the effectiveness and performance of these initiatives will show the increase (or decrease) in the maturity of the organization's controls.

5.2.3   THE CENTER FOR INTERNET SECURITY CRITICAL SECURITY CONTROLS

There are many organizations that provide timely information on what are considered to be the "top" controls. The Center for Internet Security Critical Security Controls Top 20 [formerly the SysSdmin, Audit, Network, Security (SANS)] are a recognized and widely used list of controls for cyber defense. The CIS controls are referenced by the NIST CSF as a recommended implementation approach, and are broken down by three categories: Basic, Foundational, and Organizational. All cyber programs should include the majority of these controls.

5.2.4   AUDITING OF INFORMATION TECHNOLOGY (IT) CONTROLS

Auditing of IT controls is an important and critical process that assesses the organization's control maturity posture. A controls assessment is an extremely useful tool in identifying gaps and areas for improvement.

IT controls are procedures, policies, and activities that are conducted to meet IT objectives, manage risks, comply with regulations, and conform to standards. IT controls should be implemented in all critical aspects of IT operations. IT controls can provide reasonable assurance that the information technology utilized by an organization functions as intended, that data is reliable, and that the organization is in compliance with applicable laws and regulations.

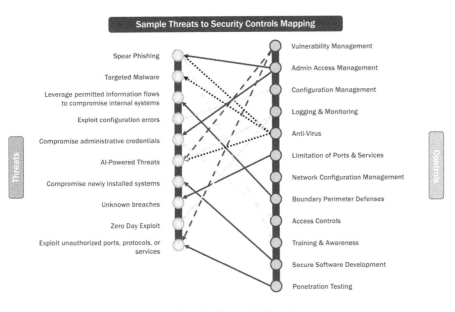

FIGURE 5.12   Sample Threats to Security Controls Mapping.

There are a number of ways that the maturity and efficacy of controls can be audited. The following bodies and/or organizations can perform an IT audit:

- Internal Audit
- External Audit
- A Regulatory Agency
- A Third Party Consultancy
- Self-Assessment by the Business Unit

After the audit, a report should be prepared to identify the particular findings of the audit and recommendations going forward. The results of the audit can be one of the most effective ways to spark senior management in initiating new projects and programs, without waiting for a security breach or attack to get their attention.

After an assessment of controls, the typical cyber threats can then be mapped to critical security controls. This is an important exercise. An example of such a mapping is shown in Figure 5.12.

5.3   CYBER INSURANCE

Cyber risk or cyber liability insurance covers (to a limit) a business' liability for a data breach where the company's customer information is exposed, stolen, or ransomed. Cyber insurance can help protect businesses from major expenses, including business losses, regulatory fines, and penalties (where insurable). It is strongly advised that companies explore and potentially purchase cyber insurance, especially if they process financial or health data, or if they have data assets that are critical to the operation of the company. Typical areas to be covered in a Cyber Insurance Policy are listed below:

1. Breach Notice Coverage and Response
2. Reputational Harm
3. Increased Credit Monitoring
4. Identity Theft Remediation
5. Cyber, Privacy, and Security Liability
6. Cyber Incident Response
7. Cyber Business Interruption
8. Digital Data Recovery
9. Cyber and Network Extortion
10. Hacker Damage
11. Increased Public Relations efforts
12. Regulatory Liability

In today's operating world, cyber insurance is likely seen as an imperative investment as it allows additional protections – both financial and response assistance – in the event of a cyber breach. The financial aspect is straightforward: if a company has a data breach or suffers a loss of operations due to a cyberattack, the insurance will step in and provide financial assistance. The nonobvious area where cyber insurance is worthwhile is the breach response services that cyber insurance companies can provide. These services can help with indecision during crisis periods and provide needed relief when organizations may not be mature enough to have developed and tested disaster recovery plans. A great aspect about the breach response services is that they are not just for data breaches like the name suggests, but for business continuity assistance as well. Additionally, the legal services network that an insurance company can provide can be of great value if a serious cyberattack occurs.

5.3.1 RISK TRANSFER

As Figure 5.13 shows, the concept of risk transfer is the main benefit organizations can get by purchasing cyber insurance. The figure shows an organization that has decent understanding and management of its cyber security and cyber resilience risks, but it has opted against purchasing cyber insurance. Due to this decision, the organization leaves some of their risks uncovered. As we see in the following example, this very same organization, with decent understanding and management of its cybersecurity and cyber resiliency risks, has more coverage if a cyber event were to occur because it has opted to purchase cyber insurance. The risks that organization knew of – or may not have known of, but had no control over – were effectively transferred from the organization to the insurance company. Obviously, this comes with a price and it is up to the organization to decide if the price of cyber insurance is worth the benefits that partnering with an insurance company grants an organization. Of course, not all risks can be transferred. Having cyber insurance does not guarantee full and complete coverage from any cyber event occurring and should not be treated that way – cyber insurance may not reduce the likelihood of a risk occurring. It is designed to lessen the impact if an event does occur.

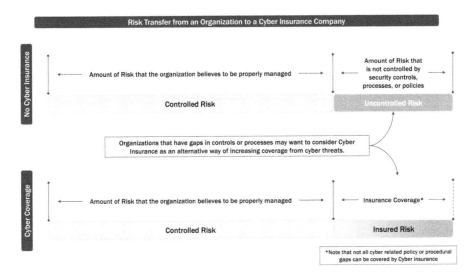

FIGURE 5.13 Cyber Insurance Risk Transfer.

NOTES

1. Source: The Risk IT Framework ©2009. ISACA. All rights reserved. Used by Permission.
2. Source: The Risk IT Framework ©2009. ISACA. All rights reserved. Used by Permission.
3. ISO/ISEC International Organization for Standardization (ISO) and the International Electrotechnical Commission (IEC).
4. Source: FAIR Textbook: Measuring and Managing Information Risk, 1st Edition, Published Aug 2014. Permission given by author Jack Freund, PHD, RiskLens.
5. Carnegie Mellon University, Software Engineering Institute
   - This publication incorporates portions of Technical Report, "Risk Management Framework" by Christopher J. Alberts and Audrey J. Dorofee, CMU/SEI-2010-TR-017 © 2010 Carnegie Mellon University, with special permission from its Software Engineering Institute.
   - Any material of Carnegie Mellon University and/or its software engineering institute contained herein is furnished on an "as-is" basis. Carnegie Mellon University makes no warranties of any kind, either expressed or implied, as to any matter including, but not limited to, warranty of fitness for purpose or merchantability, exclusivity, or results obtained from use of the material. Carnegie Mellon University does not make any warranty of any kind with respect to freedom from patent, trademark, or copyright infringement.
   - This publication has not been reviewed nor is it endorsed by Carnegie Mellon University or its Software Engineering Institute.
6. Source: The Risk IT Framework ©2009. ISACA. All rights reserved. Used by Permission.
7. Source: The Risk IT Framework ©2009. ISACA. All rights reserved. Used by Permission.
8. Source: Open Web Application Security Project™ OWASP Foundation.
9. Source: ©2017 Committee of Sponsoring Organizations of the Treadway Commission (COSO).
10. Source: FAIR Textbook: Measuring and Managing Information Risk, 1st Edition, Published Aug 2014. Permission given by author Jack Freund, PHD, RiskLens.
11. Source: FAIR Textbook: Measuring and Managing Information Risk. Permission given by author Jack Freund, PHD, RiskLens. FAIR Textbook, Chapter 12--Risk Management 2015 Measuring and Managing Information Risk.

6 Current and Target State Assessments

6.1 INTRODUCTION TO ASSESSMENTS

The assessment cycle is a lengthy and complex process that consists of planning for an assessment, evaluating the risks, responding to the risks and the assessment, and monitoring the risks and mitigations on an ongoing basis. Figure 6.1 shows a high-level general risk assessment process that will guide this chapter.

The diagram shows that the assessment process is comprised of a few stages: Plan, Assess, Respond, and Monitor. The planning phase outlines the steps and time period where risk-based decisions are being made. During this stage, various assumptions are gathered, constraints are considered, risk tolerance is loosely defined, priorities critiqued, and business processes or supply chains reviewed. The planning phase is covered more in detail in Chapter 2, but an important area to emphasize about the planning phase as it relates to assessments is to ensure that at a minimum the following questions are considered:

- What types of assessment(s) do we need?
- What types of assessment(s) can we afford?
- Are we subject to any laws or regulations that require us to do certain assessments or audits?
- Should we audit or assess any critical service providers?

Next in the cycle is is the assessment phase. This chapter will serve as the in-depth guide to assessments. This chapter will discuss the different types of assessments, the types of assessment vehicles available, and the differences between the types. Additionally, details will be provided to explain the difference between a current state assessment, a target state assessment, and how to use the products of a gap

FIGURE 6.1   Risk Assessment Process.

analysis from a target state assessment. Another important element that will be covered is the reporting on an assessment and how an assessment can be an input and a guide in forming the direction of the strategy. Next is the response phase. The response phase is how will management respond to the assessment – in the format of a formal response, designing mitigations, creating new initiatives, and prioritizing projects.

Following the assessment and response phases is the monitoring phase. This phase can be quite complex as it is not just a sustainment or simple monitoring. The monitoring phase is comprised of awareness, readiness, project management to achieve the target state, and identifying and preparing any additional assessments that may need to be completed in the future.

6.2   CURRENT STATE ASSESSMENTS

Current state assessments are an "as-is" or "point-in-time" assessment of the organization's current capabilities, current processes, and current controls. Organizations conduct current state assessments to test themselves by answering similar questions to these:

- How are our cybersecurity or cyber resiliency capabilities?
- How do our capabilities compare to our peers?
- Is there anything we can do better that will have large benefits?
- What risks are we missing?

6.2.1   CATEGORIES OF ASSESSMENTS

As mentioned, there are different categories of assessments. It will be up to the organization to determine what type of assessment is right for the current need.

TABLE 6.1
Assessment Categories

Assessment Types	Description
A. Self-Assessments	Assessments or reviews conducted "in-house" by personnel employed by the organization; can be the very group being assessed. Very few, if any, outside resources involved.
B. External/Third-Party Assessments	Assessments or reviews conducted by external third-parties. These assessments use internal resources as subject matter experts (SMEs), but are largely external staffs conducting the assessments. These groups are often comprised of consultants or contractors.
C. Audits	
a. Internal	Internal Audit: An assessment or formal audit conducted by a group outside of the department (but within the organization) being audited whose mission is to develop a formal opinion.
b. External	External Audit: In the case of an external audit, outside contractors/consultants who are qualified auditors and are the group developing the formal opinion. In both cases the audit must be responded to by senior management.

This will depend on a number of factors, but most importantly applicable resources and relevant advisory from the legal or compliance areas. Resources should be considered from the perspective of both budget availability and the skill set of in-house personnel. Legal and compliance should be consulted from the perspective of the requirements; some compliance requirements may mandate an outside assessment or audit. Table 6.1 gives a light introduction to the different types of assessments while Table 6.2 shows some of the major assessment vehicles that an organization can be assessed against. In the following sections each category is further elaborated upon.

6.2.1.1   Self-Assessments

A self-assessment is a great first start in order to understand a company's current state. A self-assessment can be broad, it can be tailored, and it can be utilized to compare the organization to anything that the organization wishes to compare itself to. The flexibility, the ease, and the relatively low amount of resources (hence cost) required are the main benefits to conducting a self-assessment. While self-assessments are great for internal gap assessments or to track progress, they often are not considered as "in depth" or fully relied upon due to their lack of independence or expertise in the field of the assessment or potential bias. For example, if an audit is requested by the board of directors (or an equivalent) in order to determine the security posture of the organization, a self-assessment will be reviewed by the auditors, but may not be relied upon by the internal or external auditors. The internal

TABLE 6.2

Major Assessment Vehicles: Frameworks, Industry Standards, Regulations, and Models

Frameworks	Description
a. COBIT 5	COBIT 5 incorporates the latest thinking in enterprise governance and management techniques, and provides globally accepted principles, practices, analytical tools, and models to help increase the trust in, and value from, information systems.
b. Financial Services Sector Cybersecurity Profile	The Profile is a scalable and extensible assessment that financial institutions of all types can use for internal and external cyber risk management assessment and as a mechanism to evidence compliance with various regulatory frameworks both within the US and globally.
c. ISO/IEC 27001	ISO/IEC 27001 is an information security management system. It requires that management understand the risks facing their organization, develop controls accordingly, and adopt an overarching management process to ensure that the information controls continue to meet the organization's information security needs on an ongoing basis.
d. NIST CSF	The NIST CSF consists of standards, guidelines, and best practices to manage cybersecurity related risk. The CSF is notable for its prioritized, flexible, and cost-effective approach to promoting the protection and resilience. The NIST CSF is defined by the 5 functions: Identify, Protect, Detect, Respond, and Recover. The NIST CSF can be used as an assessment vehicle in a multitude of ways. It can be used as an internal gap analysis tool, it can be used by external assessors to develop a report and to establish a roadmap forward, or it can be used in an official audit. However, there is no such thing as being "NIST CSF certified" the audit report will generally measure the organization's progress against the organization's own defined goals.
e. NIST Risk Management Framework	The NIST Risk Management Framework (RMF) provides a process that integrates security and risk management activities into the system development life cycle. The NIST RMF has the following steps: Categorize System, Select Controls, Implement Controls, Assess Controls, Authorize System, and Monitor Controls. The NIST RMF can be used for internal reviews of processes, internal or external assessments, but is only used in an audit fashion to ensure processes were followed.
• FIPS 199 Categorization	FIPS 199 is the Standards for Security Categorization of Federal Information and Information Systems. The NIST RMF step of Categorize System is based upon FIPS 199. FIPS 199 Categorizes Information Systems based on perceived impact, for Confidentiality, Integrity, and Availability. It is important to note FIPS 199 is not so much an assessment vehicle as it a necessary resource within an assessment.

(Continued)

TABLE 6.2 *(Continued)*
Major Assessment Vehicles: Frameworks, Industry Standards, Regulations, and Models

Frameworks	Description
• NIST 800-53 Control Catalog	The NIST 800-53 Control Catalog, officially known as the Security and Privacy Controls for Federal Information Systems and Organizations, is one of the most well-known control catalogs within the cybersecurity world. The NIST RMF step of Select Controls and Implement Controls utilizes the NIST 800-53 control catalog. The control catalog relies on the underlying system categorization of FIPS 199. It is then up to the organization to use NIST 800-53 as a control catalog and implement the controls accordingly. The controls are customizable and implemented as part of an organization-wide process that manages information security and privacy risk.
f. CERT©-CRR	The Cyber Resilience Review (CRR) is a technical assessment to evaluate an organization's operational resiliency cybersecurity practices.
g. COSO ERM Framework	The COSO Enterprise Risk Management (ERM) Framework is usable by management to evaluate and improve their organization's ERM. This framework expands on internal controls and provides a more robust and in-depth focus on ERM.
Industry Standards	
a. PCI-DSS	The PCI-DSS was developed to encourage and enhance cardholder data security and facilitate the broad adoption of consistent data security for credit card information globally. While the PCI-DSS can be used to conduct an internal current state assessment and used to understand gaps, an official PCI-DSS assessment must be conducted by an external qualified security assessor (QSA) who then publishes a record compliance (RoC).
b. CPMI-IOSCO	The Committee on Payments and Market Infrastructures (CPMIs) and the Board of the International Organization of Securities Commissions (IOSCO) developed a Guidance on cyber resilience for financial market infrastructures (FMIs). The main goal of the guidance is to increase the FMIs' ability to predict and respond to cyberattacks, while achieving faster and safer target recovery objectives if the attacks do succeed. Additionally, these goals are meant to be country agnostic and allow each country to build resilience.
Regulations	
a. NYDFS Cyber Regulation	The New York Department of Financial Services Cybersecurity Requirements for Financial Services Companies is "designed to promote the protection of customer information as well as the information technology systems of regulated entities". An important aspect of the regulation is that it requires each regulated entity conducts a risk assessment and then implements a program with appropriate security controls.

(Continued)

TABLE 6.2 *(Continued)*

Major Assessment Vehicles: Frameworks, Industry Standards, Regulations, and Models

Models	Description
a. CMMI	Capability Maturity Model Integration (CMMI) is a model that provides guidance for developing or improving processes that meet the business goals of an organization. This model is important for measuring strategy performance as it is crucial to understand a cyber program current state maturity level vs. a target state maturity level as it relates to processes.
	The maturity rankings range from a level 1, which would be the most basic of program, to a level 5, which is the most mature level. At a level 5, a focus is placed on process improvement.
	1. Initial: Processes unpredictable, poorly controlled and reactive
	2. Managed: Processes characterized for projects and is often reactive
	3. Defined: Processes characterized for the organization and is proactive
	4. Quantitatively Managed: Processes measured and controlled
	5. Optimizing: Focus on process improvement
b. PMBOK®	The Project Management Body of Knowledge (PMBOK®) is the authoritative documentation of good practices in project management and is the basis for certification examinations to qualify Project Management Professionals (PMPs). The body of knowledge is organized into 5 process groups that comprise of a total of 47 project management processes. Each of the 47 processes consists of Inputs, Tools and Techniques, and Outputs. Separately, the 47 process are also grouped into 10 different project management knowledge areas.
c. CERT©-RMM	Resilience Management Model (RMM) is the foundation for a process-improvement approach to operational resilience management.
d. FAIR	Factor Analysis of Information Risk (FAIR) is a methodology for quantifying and managing risk in any organization. The FAIR methodology allows organizations to understand, analyze, and quantify cyber risk in financial terms.
e. CM RQM	The Carnegie Mellon Risk Quantification Method (CM RQM) is a risk-based methodology of scoring and ranking initiatives based on an amount of risk reduction.

or external auditors will wish to establish independence from the development or the execution of the business functions in order to develop a non-biased opinion. There will be more information on the independence of audits in the Audit section. Perhaps the best and most well-known function of a self-assessment is a "gap analysis". A gap analysis is a very simple way to assess the organization against an industry standard (e.g., framework, model, regulation), a best practice, or a compliance requirement in a short amount of time. The gap analysis is conducted by making high-level yes or no answers as to whether or not the organization is meeting the industry standard, compliance requirement, or is mirroring best practices. This provides a quick judgment of how the organization's processes may compare, but only uses the opinion of the subject matter experts and evidence collection is generally optional in order to keep the resource requirements low.

6.2.1.2 External/Third-Party Assessments

The next category of an assessments is external assessments, often referred to as third-party assessments. As mentioned earlier in Table 6.1, external assessments are conducted by resources external to the organization, usually in the form of contractors or consultants. External assessors are usually chosen due to their expertise with the subject matter being assessed. For example, an external assessor that is highly specialized and experienced with the payment card industry data security standard (PCI-DSS) requirements is likely the best choice in order to conduct an assessment of the organization's readiness for a PCI-DSS audit. When it comes to independence and the formulation of an opinion, external assessors may either use a "trust but verify" approach or may rely on the work of a self-assessment. It generally depends upon the scope of the individual external assessment and the organization requesting the external assessment's wishes and budget as to the depth and breadth of the assessment.

6.2.1.3 Audits (Internal & External)

Audits are very similar to self-assessments and external assessments, with one major aspect that is a key difference – the independence of the auditors, internal and external, to the organization being audited. Even in the case of internal audit, the auditors should have a chain of command that directly reports to the board. An external audit is different from an external assessment by the requirements and the attestation of the firm conducting the audit, but similar in the fact that the firm or the auditors are expected to have a particular set of expertise in order to conduct the audit. This independence from the organization being audited, in both cases, allows the auditors to have an element of professional skepticism when reviewing the organization and its performance against an assessment vehicle. For example, in the case of a PCI-DSS audit, only a qualified security assessor should be the main contact or point person of the security audit. This person (on behalf of their company) gives their official approval that all controls are effective. As mentioned in Table 6.1, both types of audits must have a senior management response. Senior management will note whether or not they agree and/or disagree with the opinion of the auditors providing justification in the form of a written response.

NIST CSF Framework Core Identifiers and Categories			
Function ID	**Function**	**Category ID**	**Category**
ID	Identify	AM	Asset Management
		BE	Business Environment
		GV	Governance
		RA	Risk Assessment
		RM	Risk Management
PR	Protect	AC	Access Control
		AT	Awareness & Training
		DS	Data Security
		IP	Information Protection
		PT	Protection Technology
DE	Detect	AE	Anomalies & Events
		CM	Security Continuous Monitoring
		DP	Detection Processes
RS	Respond	CO	Communications
		AN	Analysis
		MI	Mitigation
		IM	Improvements
RC	Recover	RP	Recovery Planning
		IM	Improvements
		CO	Communications

FIGURE 6.2   NIST CSF Framework Core Identifiers and Categories.

6.2.2 Frameworks, Industry Standards, Regulations, and Models

6.2.2.1 NIST Cybersecurity Framework Core Identifiers and Categories

Figure 6.2 shows NIST CSF Framework Core Identifiers and Categories. The functions are further broken down here for purposes of the new initiatives' derivation evaluation.

6.3   CONDUCTING A CURRENT STATE ASSESSMENT

Conducting an assessment can sometimes seem like a complex task. In order to guide this process, the NIST Cybersecurity Framework (NIST CSF) has been referred to in this book as one of the most important tools by which an assessment can be conducted. Referring back to Figure 6.2, we can map each initiative in the current Cyber Program to each NIST Functional Category. By doing so, we can further determine the areas that have and have not been addressed by the current Cyber Program. This will be one method of establishing the gaps for future initiative development. The complete mapping of the 50 listed initiatives for each of the 5 Cybersecurity and the 5 Cyber Resiliency strategic objectives have been mapped in Table 6.3. To read the mapping, note that the field "Initiative #" is used to note what domain and objective

TABLE 6.3
CSF to Cybersecurity and Cyber Resiliency Initiatives Mapping

	NIST CSF Category	Initiative #	Initiative
IDENTIFY (ID)	**Asset Management (ID.AM):** The data, personnel, devices, systems, and facilities that enable the organization to achieve business purposes are identified and managed consistent with their relative importance to organizational objectives and the organization's risk strategy.	CS.5.1	Develop and implement a comprehensive asset-protection program consisting of asset, vulnerability, patching, logging, monitoring, and alerting management modules for the complete inventory of all technology assets
		CS.5.5	Develop a standard cyber hygiene approach by implementing critical security controls
		CR.1.1	Determine the recovery requirements for the critical business units of the organization
		CR.1.3	Document the current state network architecture for critical business units and their dependencies
		CR.3.1	Evaluate supply chain chokepoints for IT services and understand critical third-party services
		CR.3.4	Develop a list of critical systems, applications, and businesses in priority order
	Business Environment (ID.BE): The organization's mission, objectives, stakeholders, and activities are understood and prioritized; this information is used to inform cybersecurity roles, responsibilities, and risk management decisions.	CS.1.3	Map the current cybersecurity strategy(s) and program(s) alignment with business needs and corporate goals
		CR.1.1	Determine the recovery requirements for the critical business units of the organization
		CR.1.3	Document the current state network architecture for critical business units and their dependencies
		CR.3.1	Evaluate supply chain chokepoints for IT services and understand critical third-party services
	Governance (ID.GV): The policies, procedures, and processes to manage and monitor the organization's regulatory, legal, risk, environmental, and operational requirements are understood and inform the management of cybersecurity risk.	CS.1.1	Perform a Risk Assessment to quantify the current state
		CS.1.2	Perform a gap analysis between current and target states to determine potential areas of additional resource investment
		CS.4.1	Develop a Cybersecurity Awareness Program
		CS.5.4	Develop a methodology of mapping assets (people, processes, technology) to initiatives in order to determine the total risk scores of each initiative
		CR.2.2	Perform various risk assessments across the current state technical architecture

(Continued)

TABLE 6.3 *(Continued)*

CSF to Cybersecurity and Cyber Resiliency Initiatives Mapping

NIST CSF Category	Initiative #	Initiative
Risk Assessment (ID.RA): The organization understands the cybersecurity risk to organizational operations (including mission, functions, image, or reputation), organizational assets, and individuals.	CS.1.4	Document all Cyber Business Risks and responses within a risk register
	CS.2.3	Perform threat modeling techniques on systems and applications to determine weak points
	CS.3.2	Using this risk-based approach, evaluate the current state risk of each asset and determine the target state risk of each asset
	CS.5.1	Develop and implement a comprehensive asset protection program consisting of asset, vulnerability, patching, logging, monitoring, and alerting management modules for the complete inventory of all technology assets
	CR.5.1	Perform a threat analysis for critical systems and high-risk areas
	CR.5.2	Create or update incident response plans based on calculated risk levels and current threats
	CR.5.3	Implement a 24/7 Incident Response Team inclusive of digital forensics
Risk Management Strategy (ID.RM): The organization's priorities, constraints, risk tolerances, and assumptions are established and used to support operational risk decisions.	CS.3.1	Select or develop a company-wide risk analysis methodology to analyze and prioritize cyber threats
Supply Chain Risk Management (ID.SC): The organization's priorities, constraints, risk tolerances, and assumptions are established and used to support risk decisions associated with managing supply chain risk. The organization has established and implemented the processes to identify, assess and manage supply chain risks.	CR.3.1	Evaluate supply chain chokepoints for IT services and understand critical third-party services

IDENTIFY (ID)

(Continued)

TABLE 6.3 *(Continued)*

CSF to Cybersecurity and Cyber Resiliency Initiatives Mapping

<table>
<tr><td colspan="2"></td><td>NIST CSF Category</td><td>Initiative #</td><td>Initiative</td></tr>
<tr><td rowspan="6">PROTECT (PR)</td><td></td><td>Identity Management, Authentication and Access Control (PR.AC): Access to physical and logical assets and associated facilities is limited to authorized users, processes, and devices, and is managed consistent with the assessed risk of unauthorized access to authorized activities and transactions.</td><td>CR.2.4</td><td>Segment the technical architecture according to risk level</td></tr>
<tr><td></td><td rowspan="5">Awareness and Training (PR.AT): The organization's personnel and partners are provided cybersecurity awareness education and are trained to perform their cybersecurity-related duties and responsibilities consistent with related policies, procedures, and agreements.</td><td>CS.4.1</td><td>Develop a Cybersecurity Awareness Program</td></tr>
<tr><td></td><td>CS.4.2</td><td>Advertise elements of the Program on the premises of the organization as well as online</td></tr>
<tr><td></td><td>CS.4.3</td><td>Implement Phishing or other tests to determine the level of compliance with the Awareness Program</td></tr>
<tr><td></td><td>CS.4.4</td><td>For those who repeatedly fail the tests, implement training courses to improve compliance and possibly a temporary reduction of system privileges</td></tr>
<tr><td></td><td>CS.4.5</td><td>Advertise group results of the tests to promote compliance</td></tr>
<tr><td></td><td rowspan="4">Data Security (PR.DS): Information and records (data) are managed consistent with the organization's risk strategy to protect the confidentiality, integrity, and availability of information.</td><td>CS.2.4</td><td>Deploy the principles of least privilege, defense in depth, and separation of duties when creating and maintaining secure Software Development Life Cycle (SDLC) environments</td></tr>
<tr><td></td><td>CS.5.5</td><td>Develop a standard cyber hygiene approach by implementing critical security controls</td></tr>
<tr><td></td><td>CR.2.5</td><td>Document and isolate any end-of-life or out of support systems and/or applications</td></tr>
<tr><td></td><td>CR.3.4</td><td>Develop a list of critical systems, applications, and businesses in priority order</td></tr>
</table>

(Continued)

TABLE 6.3 *(Continued)*

CSF to Cybersecurity and Cyber Resiliency Initiatives Mapping

	NIST CSF Category	Initiative #	Initiative
PROTECT (PR)	**Information Protection Processes and Procedures (PR.IP):** Security policies (that address purpose, scope, roles, responsibilities, management commitment, and coordination among organizational entities), processes, and procedures are maintained and used to manage protection of information systems and assets.	CS.2.1	Adopt a formal SDLC process for software design
		CS.2.5	Execute and document quality assurance protocols at every phase of the SDLC
		CS.5.1	Develop and implement a comprehensive asset protection program consisting of asset, vulnerability, patching, logging, monitoring, and alerting management modules for the complete inventory of all technology assets
		CS.5.5	Develop a standard cyber hygiene approach by implementing critical security controls
		CR.3.4	Develop a list of critical systems, applications, and businesses in priority order
		CR.3.5	Document and test against established Recovery Time Objectives (RTO) and Recovery Point Objectives (RPO)
		CR.4.1	Review any contracts with in-house providers or outside vendors regarding the provision of services in a breach situation
	Maintenance (PR.MA): Maintenance and repairs of industrial control and information system components are performed consistent with policies and procedures.	None	
	Protective Technology (PR.PT): Technical security solutions are managed to ensure the security and resilience of systems and assets, consistent with related policies, procedures, and agreements.	CS.5.1	Develop and implement a comprehensive asset protection program consisting of asset, vulnerability, patching, logging, monitoring, and alerting management modules for the complete inventory of all technology assets
		CS.5.5	Develop a standard cyber hygiene approach by implementing critical security controls
		CR.3.4	Develop a list of critical systems, applications, and businesses in priority order

(Continued)

TABLE 6.3 *(Continued)*

CSF to Cybersecurity and Cyber Resiliency Initiatives Mapping

<table>
<tr><td></td><td>Category</td><td>Initiative #</td><td>Initiative</td></tr>
<tr><td rowspan="7">DETECT (DE)</td><td rowspan="2">Anomalies and Events (DE. AE): Anomalous activity is detected and the potential impact of events is understood.</td><td>CS.1.4</td><td>Document all Cyber Business Risks and responses within a risk register</td></tr>
<tr><td>CS.5.1</td><td>Develop and implement a comprehensive asset protection program consisting of asset, vulnerability, patching, logging, monitoring, and alerting management modules for the complete inventory of all technology assets</td></tr>
<tr><td>Security Continuous Monitoring (DE.CM): The information system and assets are monitored to identify cybersecurity events and verify the effectiveness of protective measures.</td><td>CS.5.1</td><td>Develop and implement a comprehensive asset protection program consisting of asset, vulnerability, patching, logging, monitoring, and alerting management modules for the complete inventory of all technology assets</td></tr>
<tr><td>Detection Processes (DE.DP): Detection processes and procedures are maintained and tested to ensure awareness of anomalous events.</td><td>CS.5.3</td><td>Create a cyber threat intelligence program that collects and analyzes current threat information regarding cyberattacks in order to contribute to the overall asset risk calculation</td></tr>
<tr><td></td><td>Category</td><td>Initiative #</td><td>Initiative</td></tr>
<tr><td rowspan="6">RESPOND (RS)</td><td>Response Planning (RS.RP): Response processes and procedures are executed and maintained, to ensure response to detected cybersecurity incidents.</td><td>CR.3.3</td><td>Create a plan for dual site failover and recovery</td></tr>
<tr><td rowspan="3">Communications (RS.CO): Response activities are coordinated with internal and external stakeholders (e.g., external support from law enforcement agencies).</td><td>CR.3.3</td><td>Create a plan for dual site failover and recovery</td></tr>
<tr><td>CR.4.4</td><td>Schedule biannual attack and penetration tests to practice all incident response plans</td></tr>
<tr><td>CR.4.5</td><td>Participate and collaborate in industry-wide cyber resiliency industry and gaming events</td></tr>
<tr><td rowspan="3">Analysis (RS.AN): Analysis is conducted to ensure effective response and support recovery activities.</td><td>CS.5.3</td><td>Create a cyber threat intelligence program that collects and analyzes current threat information regarding cyberattacks in order to contribute to the overall asset risk calculation</td></tr>
<tr><td>CR.3.2</td><td>Perform Cyber War Gaming exercises to understand resilience and recovery of IT, processes, and businesses</td></tr>
<tr><td>CR.5.3</td><td>Implement a 24/7 Incident Response Team inclusive of digital forensics</td></tr>
</table>

(Continued)

TABLE 6.3 *(Continued)*

CSF to Cybersecurity and Cyber Resiliency Initiatives Mapping

	Category	Initiative #	Initiative
RESPOND (RS)	**Mitigation (RS.MI):** Activities are performed to prevent expansion of an event, mitigate its effects, and resolve the incident.	CS.1.4	Document all Cyber Business Risks and responses within a risk register
		CR.2.4	Segment the technical architecture according to risk level
	Improvements (RS.IM): Organizational response activities are improved by incorporating lessons learned from current and previous detection/response activities.	CR.1.2	Inventory all Resiliency, Disaster Recovery, and Business Continuity plans and procedures across the enterprise
		CR.4.4	Schedule biannual attack and penetration tests to practice all incident response plans

	Category	Initiative #	Initiative
RECOVER (RC)	**Recovery Planning (RC.RP):** Recovery processes and procedures are executed and maintained to ensure restoration of systems or assets affected by cybersecurity incidents.	CR.3.4	Develop a list of critical systems, applications, and businesses in priority order
		CR.4.3	Determine if manual processes can fulfill business needs during periods of IT unavailability
		CR.5.5	Develop a failover capability using alternate technologies to carry out business processes
	Improvements (RC.IM): Recovery planning and processes are improved by incorporating lessons learned into future activities.	CR.1.2	Inventory all Resiliency, Disaster Recovery, and Business Continuity plans and procedures across the enterprise
		CR.3.3	Create a plan for dual site failover and recovery
	Communications (RC.CO): Restoration activities are coordinated with internal and external parties (e.g., coordinating centers, Internet Service Providers, owners of attacking systems, victims, other CSIRTs, and vendors).	CR.1.4	Select an appropriate cyber insurance policy
		CR.4.1	Review any contracts with in-house providers or outside vendors regarding the provision of services in a breach situation
		CR.4.2	Physically document cyber insurance policies and contact information
		CR.5.4	Issue an RFI and select a breach response vendor

the initiative is tied to. CS means that the initiative is cybersecurity based, while CR denotes that the initiative is cyber resiliency based. The first digit following the S or R denotes what number objective the initiative is tied to, while the second digit denotes what number initiative within the objective. For example, CS.1.1 shows that the specific initiative is within the cybersecurity domain (CS), is the part of the first strategic objective (1), and the first initiative (1). Note also that some initiatives may apply to multiple domains.

By closely examining the more specific allocation of initiatives and arriving at some general conclusions regarding areas of initiative concentration, a full picture of the current Cybersecurity Program will be evident. Some conclusions here might be:

1. Dominant area of concentration seems to be Governance
2. Response and Recover are light and should be represented more
3. Communication needs to be enhanced

Although some areas are light, they might have been that way by design. Remember that we are entering the program development process midstream after past assessments and gap analyses have been completed, and program adjustments made. However, having said that, in order to augment Response, Recover, and Communication, some potential new initiatives might be:

Response and Communication:

1. Ensure an up-to-date Incident Response Plan is in effect and reviewed on a periodic basis.
2. Ensure that the Incident Response Plan contains timely communication protocols with the Stakeholders and all vendors.

Recover and Communication:

1. Perform periodic tests of the Response and Recovery Plans.
2. Ensure that all recovery activities include timely communication protocols with Stakeholders and any critical vendors.

6.4   UNMAPPED INITIATIVES DISCUSSION

Not all initiatives can be directly mapped to individual CSF capabilities. Some initiatives are too broad, some are basic management goals, or some are preparatory in nature for future projects. Tables 6.4 and 6.5 review those not mapped and provide an explanation as to why they are still important.

6.5   TARGET STATE ASSESSMENT

A target state assessment is the end goal of where the organization aspires to be. A target state can be the end goals outlined in a strategy, or it can simply be a listing of objectives or initiatives that when completed bring the organization closer to its

TABLE 6.4

Cybersecurity Initiatives NOT Mapped to the CSF

#	Initiative	Reasoning
CS.1.5	Conduct a Cost Benefit Analysis of hiring a consultancy vs. hiring in-house talent to develop the strategic plan.	This effort is good practice in keeping down costs and supplementing talent and resources where required.
CS.2.2	Ensure that security requirements are defined and documented in the business requirements gathering and analysis phase.	This is standard SDLC practice when developing any projects.
CS.3.3	Perform the gap analysis and compare the actual year end performance to the desired target state.	This exercise will provide additional information as to the performance of the plan and assist in deciding which projects should move forward, change priority, or be retired.
CS.3.4	Analyze the concentration of the initiatives within the CSF capabilities and the risk mitigation performance.	By reviewing the concentration of initiatives within each CSF capability, the organization can determine the degree of effort and resources dedicated to that area. By comparing the amount of effort spent and the resultant risk mitigation accomplishments, management may want to trim back and/or increase efforts in that area to provide additional progress.
CS.3.5	Based on the risk mitigation and target state performance goals, determine the areas of future initiative concentration.	By comparing the resultant risk mitigation with the predetermined target state goals, future CSF areas of concentration can be identified.
CS.5.2	Utilizing the company-wide risk analysis methodology selected previously, calculate the risk associated with each asset and develop specific protection protocols per asset.	Calculating asset risk is an ongoing process and is integral to designing the risk mitigation strategy. This strategy will lead to the selection and implementation of the organization's protection protocols and products.

cybersecurity and cyber resiliency maturity goals, or it may just be compliance with certain regulations. It can also be all or some of the above.

There are really two parts to the target state assessment. The first part is determining what your target is; the next part is determining the gap between the target state and the current state. (The third part would then be to figure out how to get to the target state, but more on this later.) Figure 6.3 visually outlines the steps to complete a target state assessment and the gap between the current state and the target state.

The first step in the diagram above is showing an organization that has just completed a current state assessment. While this is a good start, it is not enough as there

TABLE 6.5

Cyber Resiliency Initiatives NOT Mapped to the CSF

#	Initiative	Reasoning
CR.1.5	Align all resiliency efforts across the enterprise to gain senior management support and efficiencies of scale.	Alignment of cyber resiliency efforts is one of the main themes of this book. In this manner, business silos will get support, additional resources, and be more likely to receive top management buy-in.
CR.2.1	Design a target state technical architecture including Data, Applications, Network, and the Cloud.	Creating and maintaining a target state technical architecture should be performed routinely as it will provide the necessary information for assessing technology risk and defining corresponding security solutions, products, and controls.
CR.2.3	Inventory all resiliency and business continuity technological capabilities across the enterprise in order to gauge current cyberattack response potential.	This is critical in order to combine efforts and efficiencies. One of the main themes of this book is the importance of centralizing cyber efforts in order to provide a uniform approach, take advantage of efficiencies, and receive top management support.

is nothing with which to compare the organization's current state to. The organization understands its current maturity, but it doesn't know which goals to work towards and there is limited direction.

The second step shows an organization with a target state defined. At this stage, the organization understands what goals it wants to accomplish, and it understands a general direction in which to travel on the path to increased maturity.

The last step shows a current state assessment completed, a target state defined, and a gap analysis conducted. As is evident, this is the most complete of all the images. At this stage, the organization understands where its current state maturity is, what goals the organization has defined for itself, and through the gap analysis it understands the individual steps and tasks necessary to complete in order to achieve these overall goals.

6.5.1 NIST CSF TARGET STATES

As previously discussed in the section on current assessments, the NIST CSF has the ability to serve as an assessment vehicle to determine both a current state and a target state. The current state is simply a point in time assessment of an organization's cybersecurity and cyber resiliency capabilities, while a target state is the alignment with the framework core that the organization sees as the most appropriate fit.

The target state is often the result of many discussions with senior management due to the ramifications of the decision. By understanding where the organization falls

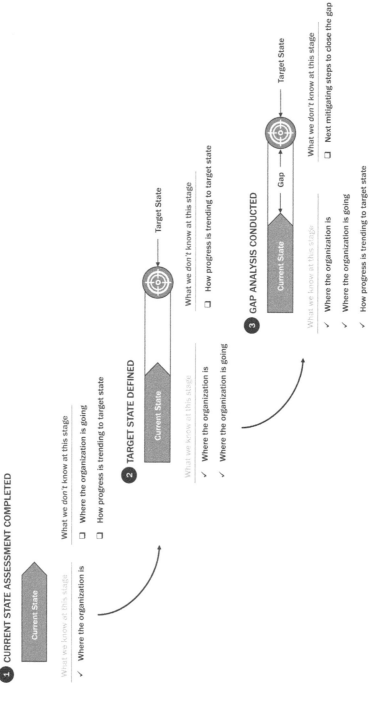

FIGURE 6.3   Steps to a Target State and Gap Analysis.

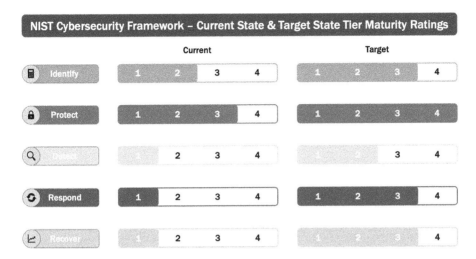

FIGURE 6.4   Cybersecurity Framework Current vs. Target State Tier Maturity Ratings.

short, or there are clear gaps with the target state, decision makers can use this information to design projects that may provide the substantial benefits within one of the five major aspects of the framework. For example, Figure 6.4 in the next section shows a sample organization's current state and target state aligned to the NIST CSF. The organization is currently on the more underdeveloped side of the scale when it comes to their cybersecurity and cyber resiliency capabilities, but they have recognized this and plan to invest accordingly. The left side of the diagram shows the current state rating for the five major categories of the CSF while the right side of the diagram shows the target state rating for the same five major categories. This sample organization feels that they need to improve across the five categories – but they do not need to improve equally across the five categories.

There are a number of factors that influence the quantification of the organization's target state's goals. This occurs naturally after the organization has performed varied assessments yielding the current state and capability gaps. Some of those factors might be:

1. The organization has committed to achieve certain goals from a regulatory, cybersecurity, cyber resiliency, audit, and customer perspectives.
2. Target goals can be shown as minimum amounts achievable for the next cycle (usually one year).
3. Examination of capability gap areas yielding weaknesses where they are not balanced
4. Whenever assessments are conducted, there are almost always gaps between the assessment vehicle/target state and the current state of the organization. At this point, it will be up to organization and project management to develop a risk and cost benefit analysis to determine if closing the gap is worthwhile. In the case of compliance requirements, often times compensating controls – when documented – are used to show compliance when gaps exist.

6.6   HOW TO RATE CURRENT AND TARGET STATES

Using the NIST CSF as an example of a framework that can be used to determine numerical ratings, organizations can arrive at a 1–4 numerical rating for the maturity level of the capability. Maturity level means how advanced (or not) the organization is at providing the capability. There are a number of ways to determine this rating:

1. Self-Assessments
2. Third-Party Assessments
3. Internal/External Audits
4. Regulatory Reviews
5. Supervisory Reviews

All of these methods utilize interviews, questionnaires, observation, and testing as their method of gathering information. Each category can be rated, and numbers combined. There can also be weightings applied. All this is left up to the organization. The important point here is to be consistent over one year's time (preferably over several years) in the method used, as otherwise there will be no basis for a true comparison between current and end-state ratings. As shown in Figure 6.4, ratings can then be compared and presented to senior management in a concise manner.

In order to assign numbers 1–4 to the CSF Current & Target State Maturity Ratings graphic, all the types of reviews mentioned above need to be taken into account in terms of CSF Tier Ratings. Table 6.6 explains all the evaluation points to be used in determining the maturity level of the organization (1–4).

TABLE 6.6
NIST CSF Tier Ratings

Tier	Description
1 – PARTIAL	*Risk Management Process*
	• Organizational cybersecurity risk management practices are not formalized, and risk is managed in an ad hoc and sometimes reactive manner.
	• Prioritization of cybersecurity activities may not be directly informed by organizational risk objectives, the threat environment, or business/mission requirements.
	Integrated Risk Management Program
	• There is limited awareness of cybersecurity risk at the organizational level. The organization implements cybersecurity risk management on an irregular, case by case basis due to varied experience or information gained from outside sources.
	• The organization may not have processes that enable cybersecurity information to be shared within the organization.

(Continued)

TABLE 6.6 *(Continued)*
NIST CSF Tier Ratings

Tier	Description
1 – PARTIAL (*continued*)	*External Participation*
	• The organization does not understand its role in the larger ecosystem with respect to either its dependencies or dependents.
	• The organization does not collaborate with or receive information from other entities, nor does it share information.
	• The organization is generally unaware of the cyber supply chain risks of the products and services it provides and that it uses.
2 – RISK INFORMED	*Risk Management Process*
	• Risk management practices are approved by management but may not be established as organizational-wide policy.
	• Prioritization of cybersecurity activities is directly informed by organizational risk objectives, the threat environment, or business/mission requirements.
	Integrated Risk Management Program
	• There is an awareness of cybersecurity risk at the organizational level, but an organization-wide approach to managing cybersecurity risk has not been established.
	• Cybersecurity information is shared within the organization on an informal basis.
	• Consideration of cybersecurity in organizational objectives and programs may occur at some but not all levels of the organization.
	• Cyber risk assessment of organizational and external assets occurs but is not typically repeatable or reoccurring.
	External Participation
	• Generally, the organization understands its role in the larger ecosystem with respect to either its own dependencies or dependents, but not both.
	• The organization collaborates with and receives some information from other entities and generates some of its own information but may not share information with others.
	• Additionally, the organization is aware of the cyber supply chain risks associated with the products and services it provides and uses but does not act consistently or formally upon those risks.
3 – REPEATABLE	*Risk Management Process*
	• The organization's risk management practices are formally approved and expressed as policy.
	• Organizational cybersecurity practices are regularly updated based on the application of risk management processes to changes in business/mission requirements and a changing threat and technology landscape.

(Continued)

TABLE 6.6 *(Continued)*
NIST CSF Tier Ratings

Tier	Description
3 – REPEATABLE *(continued)*	*Integrated Risk Management Program*
	• There is an organization-wide approach to manage cybersecurity risk. Risk-informed policies, processes, and procedures are defined, implemented as intended, and reviewed.
	• Consistent methods are in place to respond effectively to changes in risk. Personnel possess the knowledge and skills to perform their appointed roles and responsibilities.
	• The organization consistently and accurately monitors cybersecurity risk of organizational assets.
	• Senior cybersecurity and non-cybersecurity executives communicate regularly regarding cybersecurity risk. Senior executives ensure consideration of cybersecurity through all lines of operation in the organization.
	External Participation
	• The organization understands its role, dependencies, and dependents in the larger ecosystem and may contribute to the community's broader understanding of risks. It collaborates with and receives information from other entities regularly that complements internally generated information, and shares information with other entities.
	• The organization is aware of the cyber supply chain risks associated with the products and services it provides and that it uses. Additionally, it usually acts formally upon those risks, including mechanisms such as written agreements to communicate baseline requirements, governance structures (e.g., risk councils), and policy implementation and monitoring.
4 – ADAPTIVE	*Risk Management Process*
	• The organization adapts its cybersecurity practices based on previous and current cybersecurity activities, including lessons learned and predictive indicators.
	• Through a process of continuous improvement incorporating advanced cybersecurity technologies and practices, the organization actively adapts to a changing threat and technology landscape and responds in a timely and effective manner to evolving, sophisticated threats.
	Integrated Risk Management Program
	• There is an organization-wide approach to managing cybersecurity risk that uses risk-informed policies, processes, and procedures to address potential cybersecurity events.
	• The relationship between cybersecurity risk and organizational objectives is clearly understood and considered when making decisions.
	• Senior executives monitor cybersecurity risk in the same context as financial risk and other organizational risks.

(Continued)

TABLE 6.6 *(Continued)*
NIST CSF Tier Ratings

Tier	Description
4 – ADAPTIVE *(continued)*	• The organizational budget is based on an understanding of the current and predicted risk environment and risk tolerance.
	• Business units implement executive vision and analyze system-level risks in the context of the organizational risk tolerances.
	• Cybersecurity risk management is part of the organizational culture and evolves from an awareness of previous activities and continuous awareness of activities on their systems and networks.
	• The organization can quickly and efficiently account for changes to business/mission objectives in how risk is approached and communicated.
	External Participation
	• The organization understands its role, dependencies, and dependents in the larger ecosystem and contributes to the community's broader understanding of risks.
	• It receives, generates, and reviews prioritized information that informs continuous analysis of its risks as the threat and technology landscapes evolve. The organization shares that information internally and externally with other collaborators.
	• The organization uses real-time or near real-time information to understand and consistently act upon cyber supply chain risks associated with the products and services it provides and that it uses. Additionally, it communicates proactively, using formal (e.g., agreements) and informal mechanisms to develop and maintain strong supply chain relationships.

In order to arrive at the final number, the results of all the reviews and assessments mentioned at the beginning of Section 6.6 will need to be analyzed and collectively assigned a 1-4 number per CSF Capability. In this fashion, Figure 6.4 Cybersecurity Framework Current vs. Target States Tier Maturity Ratings graphic can be completed and presented to senior management in a quarterly or yearly progress report. This will be an important part of measuring strategy performance going forward.

7 Measuring Strategic Plan Performance and End of Year (EoY) Tasks

6 | Strategic Plan Performance Measurement & EoY Tasks

Measuring the performance of the strategy can be complex. There are many factors at work. The organization's existing security programs and initiatives (before the strategy was launched) may be responsible for some of the good results. It will be difficult to explicitly attribute an increase (or decrease) in the overall level of security due solely to the first year's strategy. However, there are a number of measurement methods, that when examined as a whole, can give a good overall picture as to the progress. They are:

1. Evaluating the strategy against the critical success factors in order to determine the present state concurrence
2. Checking alignment of the strategy with corporate business objectives and other existing and/or planned corporate strategies
3. Evaluating the progress of the individual initiatives/projects that comprise the strategic objectives
4. Measuring the improvement in audit, assessment, or self-assessment results that have been performed at pre-determined intervals
5. Measuring the decrease (increase) in the gap between the current state and the target state
6. Documenting the one-to-many or many-to-many correlations between the initiatives and the strategic objectives to demonstrate efficacy
7. Measuring the closing (opening) of related audit and/or cybersecurity and cyber resiliency findings

8. Utilizing the Key Risk Indicators (KRIs) that have been developed by the enterprise to calculate if overall risk has decreased
9. Utilizing the Key Performance Indicators (KPIs) that have been developed by the enterprise to calculate if overall cybersecurity and cyber resiliency has improved

Some of these points will now be gone into further detail below.

7.1 EVALUATING THE STRATEGY AGAINST THE CRITICAL SUCCESS FACTORS

The critical success factors were derived during the strategy planning phase in STEP 2, shown in Table 7.1.

Review each of the success factors and evaluate the target state results. Compare them to the original (current state) results and note the differences.

7.2 KEY RISK INDICATORS (KRIs)

The residual risk can be determined by the KRIs discussed in STEP 5. Shown again in Table 7.2 is a list of sample KRIs for cybersecurity and cyber resiliency that can be used. KRIs provide an early warning system to senior management that the goals are not being met. These indicators can be calculated on a quarterly or yearly basis and presented to senior management.

As shown in Chapter 2, the Cyber KRIs can also be presented graphically as shown in Figure 7.1.

7.3 KEY PERFORMANCE INDICATORS (KPIs)

As stated, one method to create a KRI is to identify the target implementation to be measured (e.g., the number of BUs that have adopted the cyber strategy) and the % increase against target and % change over a time unit (e.g., quarterly, yearly).

A KPI on the other hand takes the raw number of a target and measures it, then shows the % progress toward completion and % change over time unit (e.g., quarterly, yearly). A KPI should be based on quantifiable measures, showing performance goals of the organization. Table 7.3 outlines sample KPIs and explains the way that KPIs can measure trends within an organization's cybersecurity or cyber resiliency program.

As with the KRIs, the KPIs can be shown graphically as in Figure 7.2.

TABLE 7.1
Critical Success Factors

• Reduce residual risk	• Maintain budgetary constraints
• Completed by due date	• Supported by senior management
• Meets stated objectives or requirements	• Efficient use of resources
• Compliant with relevant regulations, standards, and policies	• Approved by all parties
	• Maps to corporate goals
• Reduce opportunity cost	• Aligns with approved cyber strategies

---

TABLE 7.2
Sample Key Risk Indicators (KRIs)

Key Risk Indicator	Unit of Measurement	Progress
Incident Response	Mean time to detect and respond	% increase/decrease
Security Architecture	# of BUs adopting a cyber resilient architecture	% increase/decrease
Key Controls Adoption	# of key security controls implemented yearly	% increase/decrease
Audit Findings	% increase/decrease in # of cyber-related audit findings	% findings closed out of total; % increase in findings
Threat Intelligence	Increase/decrease in quality and quantity of threat intelligence	# Alerts responded to in a timely basis as a % of the whole
Third Party Risk Management	# of business partners seen as generally effective	% increase/decrease
Security Awareness	% of employees completed cyber security training	% increase/decrease total # of employees
Regulations and Compliance	% of mandatory regulations complied with this year	% increase/decrease of total required regulations

TABLE 7.3
Sample Cyber Key Performance Indicators (KPIs)

Key Performance Indicator	Unit of Measurement	Progress
Cybersecurity Strategy	% of BUs adoption of the strategy out of total applicable BUs	% increase/decrease from last year
Cyber Resiliency Strategy	% of BUs adoption of the strategy out of total applicable BUs	% increase/decrease from last year
Threat Exposure	Documenting high-risk categories % increase in high-risk categories/year	% high-risk categories addressed
Assessments and Penetration Tests	# of critical applications and systems tested and/or assessed as a % of total required	% increase/decrease
Audit Findings	% increase/decrease in # of cyber-related audit findings	% findings closed; % increase/decrease of new findings
Patch Management	# of security patches applied as % of total required	% increase/decrease in vulnerabilities
Privileged Accounts	# of privileged accounts removed	% increase/decrease in privileged accounts
Unauthorized Access	# of unauthorized access attempts	% increase/decrease of attempts

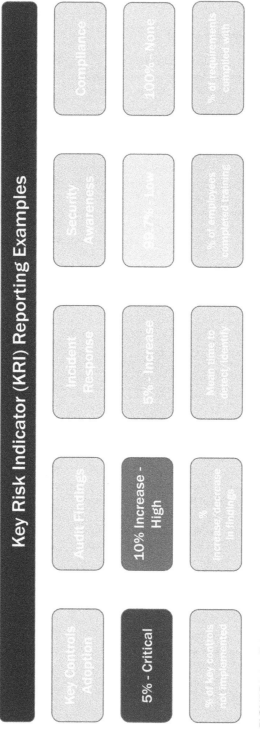

FIGURE 7.1   Cyber Key Risk Indicator (KRI) Reporting Examples.

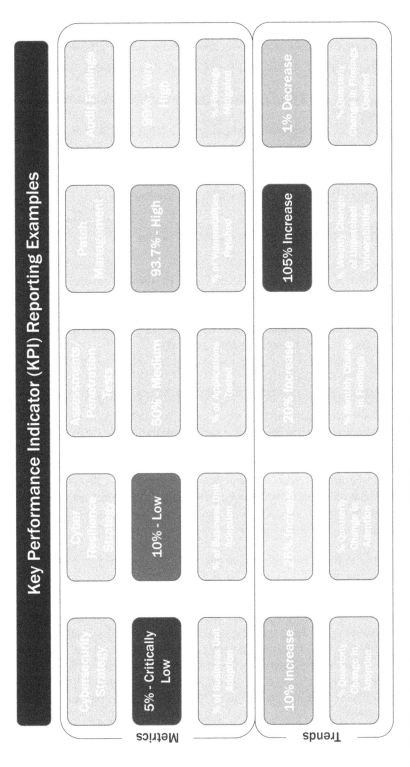

FIGURE 7.2 Cyber Key Performance Indicator (KPI) Reporting Examples.

7.4   REPORTING ON THE STRATEGIES

A variety of reports on the progress of the strategy can be prepared for senior management.

1. Cybersecurity and Cyber Resiliency Initiatives Mapped to the NIST CSF Subcategories
2. Cybersecurity Initiatives NOT Mapped to the NIST CSF Subcategories
3. Initiative to CSF Mapping per Objective
4. Strategic Plan Progress Reports – Cybersecurity and Cyber Resiliency
5. Current State to EoY and Target State Tier Rating
6. The Cybersecurity and Cyber Resiliency Yearly Report

7.4.1   CYBERSECURITY AND CYBER RESILIENCY INITIATIVES MAPPED TO NIST CSF SUBCATEGORIES

In STEP 5, Table 6.3 – Cybersecurity and Cyber Resiliency Initiatives Mapped to NIST CSF provides a very detailed mapping of Cybersecurity and Cyber Resiliency Initiatives mapped to the NIST CSF. This Table illustrates the concentration of initiatives in each of the NIST Subcategories and therefore highlighted the gaps in the current Cybersecurity and Cyber Resiliency programs.

7.4.2   CYBERSECURITY INITIATIVES NOT MAPPED TO THE NIST CSF

It is important to see which and how many initiatives contribute to each capability separately in order to determine balance and concentration. It is also important to understand which ones do not map and why. In STEP 5, Table 6.4 – Cybersecurity Initiatives NOT Mapped to the NIST CSF Subcategories presents the reasoning why some of the initiatives do not directly map to the NIST CSF. The reasoning in general is that those initiatives may be governance, procedure, or infrastructure related whose purpose is to ready the IT environment and, in many cases, should be ongoing efforts.

7.4.3   INITIATIVE TO CSF MAPPING PER OBJECTIVE

Another view of performance reporting that can be presented to senior management is to provide a series of graphics which categorize the initiatives per CSF capability that comprise each strategic objective. In this fashion, one can see the CSF capability (Identify, Protect, Detect, Respond, and Recover) concentration of the strategic objective by showing each initiative and the corresponding capabilities in which the organization is investing. As shown in Figure 7.3, an initiative can apply to one or multiple capabilities. This graphic can be replicated for each strategic objective.

Initiative to CSF Mapping per Objective					
Objective: CS.1 Develop a cybersecurity implementation plan					
#	Initiative	Identify	Protect	Detect	Respond	Recover
CS.1.1	Perform a Risk Assessment to quantify the current state	✓				
CS.1.2	Perform a gap analysis between current and target states to determine potential areas of additional resource investment	✓				
CS.1.3	Map the current cybersecurity strategy(s) and program(s) alignment with business needs and corporate goals	✓				
CS.1.4	Document all cyber business risks and responses within a risk register	✓		✓	✓	
CS.1.5	Conduct a cost benefit analysis of hiring a consultancy vs. hiring in house talent to develop the strategic plan					

FIGURE 7.3 Initiative to CSF Mapping per Objective.

7.4.4 STRATEGIC PLAN PROGRESS REPORTS – CYBERSECURITY AND CYBER RESILIENCY

Two progress reports, Figures 7.4 and 7.5, indicate the quarterly progress of each of the initiatives broken down by strategic objective. This is ideal for a periodic senior management update.

7.4.5 CURRENT STATE TO END OF YEAR AND TARGET STATE MATURITY TIER RATING

Comparing the desired Target State to the EoY State can yield general conclusions about the overall success of year one of strategy development. As we have seen in Chapter 6, Current and Target State Assessments, the organization has made progress in the following areas as shown in Figure 7.6. The coloring within the circle circumferences denotes the degree of maturity completion – a "1" being 25% filled in; a "2", being 50% filled in; a "3" being 75% filled in; and a "4" being 100% filled in. This is indicated also by the central numbers 1–4 within each circle.

Upon further examination, we can also see that there are some areas that fell short of their targets. These are the areas that may require additional resources and initiatives. The Steering Committee will need to create a dedicated subgroup to flush out what these efforts might entail.

7.4.6 PREPARATION OF THE EoY PERFORMANCE REPORT

An EoY performance report will need to go to senior management in addition to the periodic progress reports on the individual initiatives that comprise the strategic objectives. It could look something like Figure 7.7.

This sample report is divided into 4 quadrants:

1. Strategic Objection Completion: Quadrant #1 shows the % completion of the Cybersecurity and the Cyber Resiliency strategies broken down by each of the five strategic objectives. The differentiation of "On Track" to "Off Track" should be determined by Project Management Office standards. In this case, "On Track" was deemed to be 50% or more complete. Remember that objective completion can be based on many factors. Furthermore, each objective can be comprised of initiatives that are multi-year in nature in terms of duration, and therefore full completion in the current year would not be necessarily expected.

2. BU Quarterly Risk Mitigation: Quadrant #2 shows the calculated risk mitigation by BUs 1, 2, and 3 over the last 4 Quarters. The risk mitigation calculation methodology was presented in Chapter 5: Cyber Risks and Controls. A detailed spreadsheet (see Figure 5.5 Customized NIST 800-30 Cyber Risk Assessment Example) was presented that based the total risk score per asset calculation on the following factors:

   a. Assets: People, Processes, Technology
   b. Threats: Threat Rating, Probability of Occurrence, Impact Magnitude
   c. Vulnerabilities: Vulnerability Severity

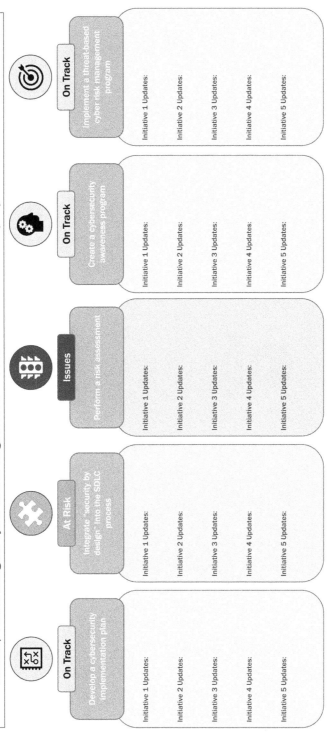

FIGURE 7.4   Strategic Plan Progress Report – Cybersecurity.

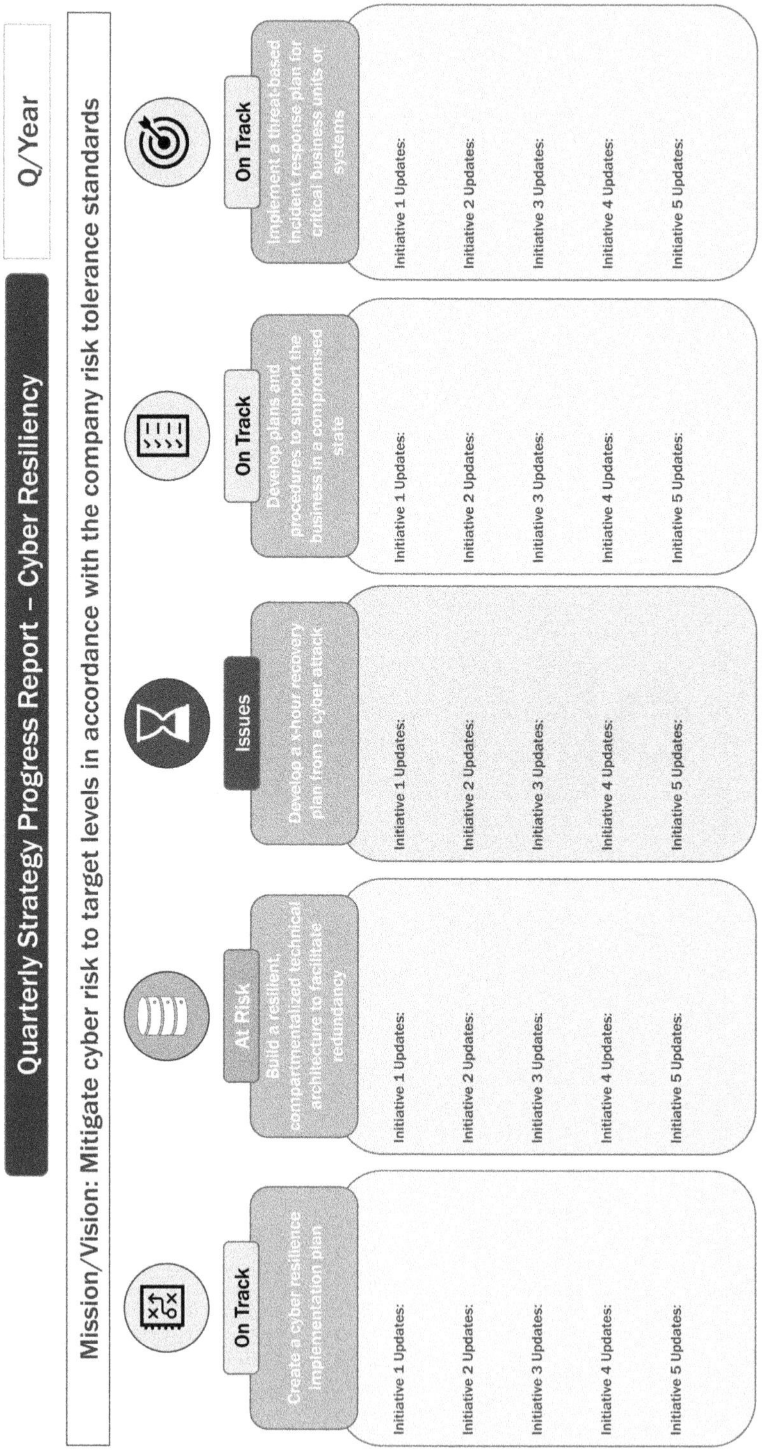

Quarterly Strategy Progress Report – Cyber Resiliency

Q/Year

Mission/Vision: Mitigate cyber risk to target levels in accordance with the company risk tolerance standards

On Track

Create a cyber resilience implementation plan

Initiative 1 Updates:

Initiative 2 Updates:

Initiative 3 Updates:

Initiative 4 Updates:

Initiative 5 Updates:

At Risk

Build a resilient, compartmentalized technical architecture to facilitate redundancy

Initiative 1 Updates:

Initiative 2 Updates:

Initiative 3 Updates:

Initiative 4 Updates:

Initiative 5 Updates:

Issues

Develop a 1-hour recovery plan from a cyber attack

Initiative 1 Updates:

Initiative 2 Updates:

Initiative 3 Updates:

Initiative 4 Updates:

Initiative 5 Updates:

On Track

Develop plans and procedures to support the business in a compromised state

Initiative 1 Updates:

Initiative 2 Updates:

Initiative 3 Updates:

Initiative 4 Updates:

Initiative 5 Updates:

On Track

Implement a threat-based incident response plan for critical business units or systems

Initiative 1 Updates:

Initiative 2 Updates:

Initiative 3 Updates:

Initiative 4 Updates:

Initiative 5 Updates:

FIGURE 7.5   Strategic Plan Progress Report – Cyber Resiliency.

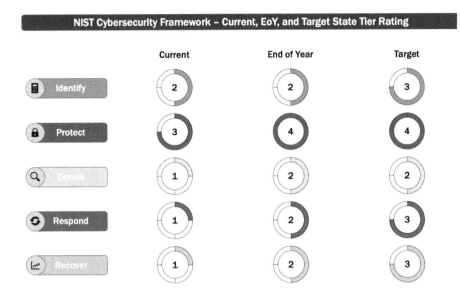

FIGURE 7.6   NIST CSF Rating: Current, End of Year (EoY), and Target States.

A calculated Total Risk Score (based on an arbitrary scale of 1–200) and subsequent assignments of High, Medium, Low (HML) were associated with each asset. Performing this calculation at successive points in time (e.g., quarterly, yearly) can yield the progress of the BU's risk mitigation. In this manner, a trend can be established as indicated by joining the points in time together in a line as shown in the graphic.

3. Cybersecurity Initiative Progress: Quadrant #3 shows the % completion of five initiatives broken down by Strategic Objective of the Cybersecurity Strategy. This graphic gives a high-level view of each cybersecurity initiative completion.

4. Cyber Resiliency Initiative Progress: Correspondingly, Quadrant #4 shows the % completion of 5 initiatives broken down by Strategic Objective of the Cyber Resiliency Strategy. As well, this graphic gives a high-level view of each Cyber Resiliency initiative completion.

7.5   DETERMINING NEW INITIATIVES FOR THE NEXT YEAR

Determining new initiatives for the following year is an extremely important outcome of the year-end strategy results. A number of factors will come into play as shown below in Figure 7.8. These inputs will be derived from STEPs 4, 5, and 6.

1. The identification of current top threats and vulnerabilities (STEP 3, Chapter 4)
2. The risk assessment results with respect to assets, people, and technology and/or any Third-Party Consultancy (STEP 4, Chapter 5)

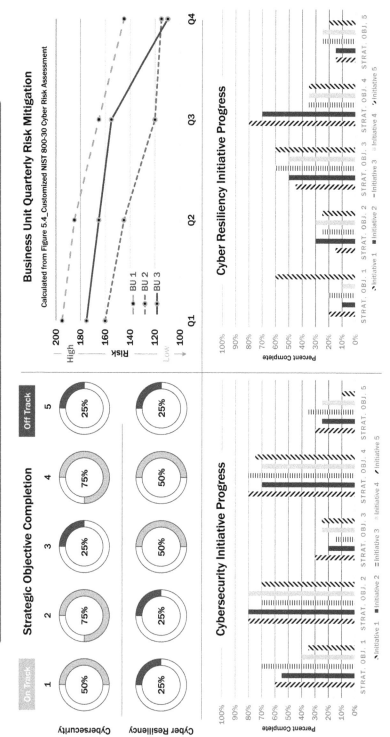

FIGURE 7.7   Cybersecurity and Cyber Resiliency Yearly Report.

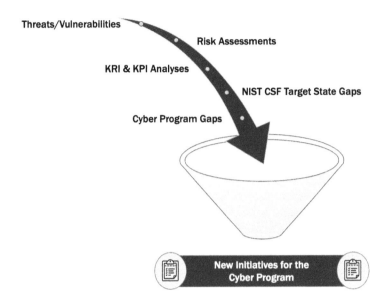

Inputs to New Initiatives

Threats/Vulnerabilities

Risk Assessments

KRI & KPI Analyses

NIST CSF Target State Gaps

Cyber Program Gaps

New Initiatives for the Cyber Program

FIGURE 7.8   Inputs to New Initiatives.

3. The KRI and KPI analyses with respect to corporate risk tolerance (STEP 4, Chapter 5)
4. The identification of Cyber Program concentration gaps (STEP 5, Chapter 6)
5. The current and actual NIST assessment results with respect to the target state numbers (STEP 5, Chapter 6)

As shown in Figure 7.8, the inputs to determine new initiatives can be illustrated graphically.

All of these factors will have to be simultaneously analyzed and depending on other factors such as corporate culture trends and budgetary constraints, a new collection and/or adjustment of strategic objectives and initiatives will be decided upon by the Steering Committee. It may also come to pass, that after an examination of underperforming initiatives, phasing out or outright cancellation may occur of some initiatives.

7.6   END OF YEAR TASKS

There will be a number of tasks that will have to be performed towards the EoY. The next sections describe those tasks.

7.6.1 Define the Strategy's Pyramid Parameters for Following Year

After all the assessments, gap analyses, and performance analyses have been completed, the Steering Committee will have to set the strategy's pyramid parameters for the following year. This will include a comprehensive review of the Mission/Vision, Principles, Strategic Objectives, and Initiatives that comprise the fundamentals of the strategy. These topics will require a lot of discussion, hence the Project Management Office (PMO) representative will need to schedule the meeting times accordingly. The individual topics can be farmed out to sub-groups and presented back to the main committee. A discussion without adequate preparation and a targeted agenda may turn into wasteful time.

7.6.2 Create the Timeline for Following Year

Lead by the PMO representative, a new timeline will need to be created for the following year. In Chapter 3, a simple strategy timeline showing progress was presented. Shown again, in Figure 7.9, now more detail can be added as a result of the previous years' experience.

Items with target dates that can be added to the overall timeline might include:

- Finalization of Mission/Vision, Principles, Objectives, and Initiatives
- Assessment of the current state
- Determination of the desired target state
- Issuance of the Quarterly Performance Reports
- Assessment of the actual target state
- Quarterly Strategy Performance Reports including conclusions regarding the progress of the strategy

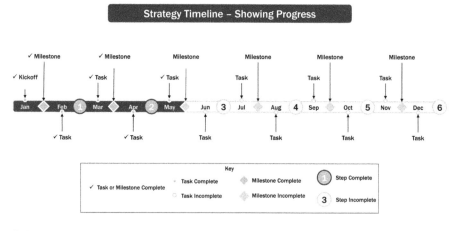

FIGURE 7.9   Strategy Timeline Showing Progress.

- Timing of the review and comment cycles of individual Governance Review Bodies on the strategy (outlined in detail in Section 7.6.7 Complete Governance Hoops)
- Date of final submission to the Board of Governors (if this is to be the last approval entity)

7.6.3   Confirm Steering Group Member Composition

Over the years, the composition of the Steering Group itself will change. This will be due to various factors such as:

- Reassignment of member participation
- Change of member responsibilities and/or job function
- Additional resource requirements
- Delegation of responsibilities
- Change in requirements of Subject Matter Experts (SMEs)
- Attrition
- New business entities joining the Committee

All of this must be taken into consideration in order to have a representative Steering Committee that will have the expertise and authority to develop and receive sanction and budget for the strategy.

7.6.4   Distribute EoY Performance Reports to Senior Management

The timely distribution of each of the performance reports to the various senior management bodies is important and advised. The Governance structure, a sample of which is shown in Figure 7.10 will need to see these reports prior to convening and with enough lead time to be able to review and comment on them.

7.6.5   End of Year Steering Committee Responsibilities RACI

There will be a number of tasks that will have to be completed toward the EoY by the Steering Committee. These tasks will be part of the master RACI (Responsible, Accountable, Consulted, or Informed) diagram and will be guided to completion by the assigned PMO.

Table 7.4 is a list of the EoY tasks for the Steering Committee. They are represented in the master RACI in STEP 2, Figures 3.10 a through e, RACI Strategy Development Matrix, which also shows their roles and responsibilities.

7.6.6   Ensure Compliance with Regulations

It is important for the Steering Committee to check with the legal, audit, and compliance departments to see if there have been any new regulations that are being developed or have been issued regarding cybersecurity and/or cyber resiliency that might affect the strategy in terms of direction in the US and also abroad that may need to be investigated. The Steering Committee will need to assign a sub-group for these tasks.

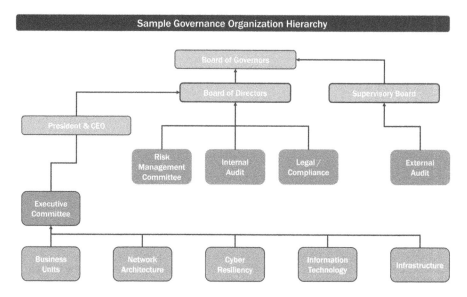

FIGURE 7.10   Sample Governance Organization Hierarchy.

7.6.7   COMPLETE GOVERNANCE HOOPS

It is best to understand the governance structure for the organization well ahead of time. Which group or committee(s) must approve the strategy? Also, these groups may not meet on a regular basis, so timing is everything. The Steering Committee will need to work closely with the PMO to arrange time on the meeting calendars well ahead of time.

TABLE 7.4
Tasks for EoY Steering Committee

- ☑ Ensure compliance with Regulations
- ☑ Prepare the EoY Strategy Performance Measurement Statistics (e.g., KRIs, KPIs, Cyber Assessment and Program gaps, initiative progress)
- ☑ Complete the Yearly Strategy Progress Report
- ☑ Determine corporate Governance requirements
- ☑ Distribute EoY reports to senior management
- ☑ Create any additional Strategy Performance Reports
- ☑ Establish objectives for the following year
- ☑ Start process for determining new initiatives for the following year
- ☑ Confirm Steering Group Committee member composition going forward
- ☑ Create timeline for the following year

7.6.7.1   Governance Organization Diagram

Prepare a Governance Organization diagram so that all Steering Committee Members can understand and confirm Governance responsibilities and determine critical approval path. Use Figure 7.10 as an example of a complex governance organization.

7.6.7.2   Strategy Governance Body RACI

Each of the governance bodies may have their own roles with respect to reviewing the strategy. Their roles may not be the same in terms of authority over the strategy. Review Figure 7.11 for some ideas about responsibilities.

NOTE: RACI: Responsible, Accountable, Consulted, or Informed (RACI). Also note that, in a RACI, only one person can be accountable, while multiple persons can have responsibility for the task. The accountable person is the individual who is ultimately answerable for the activity, while the responsible person(s) are those who actually complete the task.

7.6.7.3   Governance Approval Swimlane for the Cybersecurity and Cyber Resiliency Strategy

In order to determine the timing of the governance review cycle and the order and critical path that the strategy should take, it is recommended that a swimlane such as Figure 7.12 be created. The governance review cycle always takes longer than expected and the PMO should keep a tight rein on scheduling and tracking progress of the reviews.

On the Y-axis of the swimlane can go the individual areas/governing bodies that will need to review the strategy. They can be derived from the organizational chart, a sample of which was presented above in Figure 7.10. The flow of the review starts at the top of the swimlane and progresses down and to the right along the X-axis. The elements of the swimlane indicate if the step is a review step and/or a decision step, tracking the document as it flows along the review critical path. Note that there are many feedback loops, where comments were made by a governance body that need to be addressed by the Steering Committee. After the comments are integrated and the document updated, the cycle begins again.

In some organizations, multiple governance bodies can review the document in tandem. This is for the Steering Committee and the PMO to decide based on authorities. This way, revisions are kept to a smaller number, and the cycle itself is shorter timewise.

7.6.8   CYBERSECURITY AND CYBER RESILIENCY STRATEGY LIFE CYCLE

As illustrated again by presenting Figure 7.13, the life cycle of a strategy document is a continuous flow. The phases of Assessment, Strategy Creation, Performance Management, and New Initiative Establishment are repetitive processes. The strategy itself is a living document and together with all the tools presented in this book can continue to guide your enterprise's cybersecurity and cyber resiliency program from a risk-based perspective for many years.

GOVERNANCE ROLES RACI

STEPS & TASKS	Business Units	Steering Committee	Executive Committee	Risk Mgmt. Committee	Internal Audit	Legal / Compliance	External Audit	President & CEO	Board of Directors	Supervisory Board	Board of Governors
Develop the Cybersecurity and Cyber Resiliency Strategy	A,R	A	R	R	C	C	C	I	I	I	I
Review/Comment on the Cybersecurity and Cyber Resiliency Strategy	R	I	R	R	C	C	C	A,R	I	I	I
Review/Comment and approve the Cybersecurity and Cyber Resiliency Strategy	C	C	C	C	C	C	C	R	R	R	A,R

* Business Units role assignments are equivelent to roles for Network Architecture, Cyber Resiliency, Information Technology, Infrastructure and any other business unit contributing to the development of the strategy under the Steering Committee

FIGURE 7.11   Strategy Governance Bodies RACI.

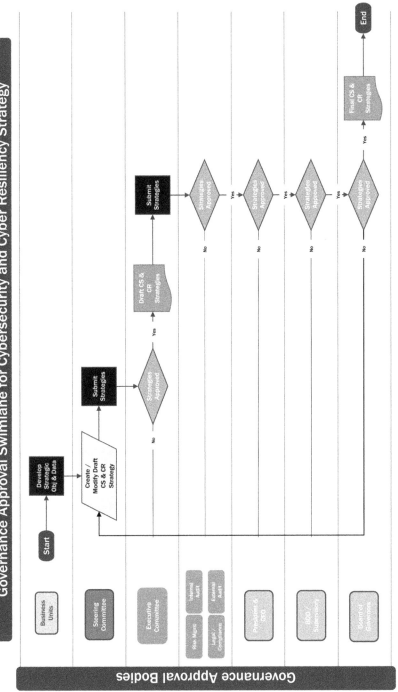

FIGURE 7.12   Governance Approval Swimlane.

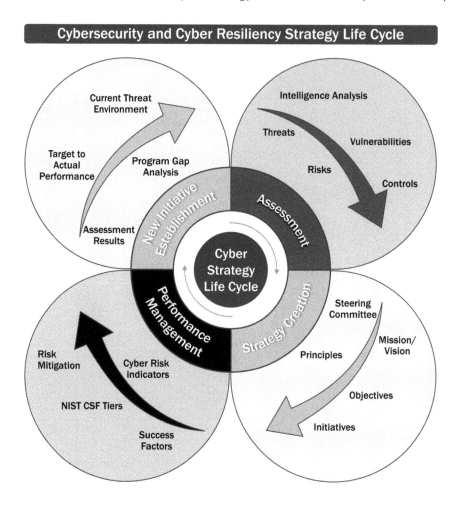

FIGURE 7.13   Cybersecurity and Cyber Resiliency Strategy Life Cycle.

8 Checklists and Templates to Help Create an Enterprise-Wide Cybersecurity and Cyber Resiliency Strategy

Figure 8.1 shows the six Development and Maintenance STEPs for a Cybersecurity and Cyber Resiliency Strategy. This chapter provides checklists, templates, process diagrams sample architectures, and RACI (Responsible, Accountable, Consulted, or Informed) spreadsheets to help create the specific strategy details that apply to your organization.

8.1 GUIDES TO STRATEGY PREPARATION

In this chapter, each of the STEPs in the 6 STEP process will have suggestions to promote thought and provide a starting point for discussion for the Steering Committee, their delegates, or any group that is charged with writing the cyber strategy. One or more of the following STEPs can be useful in your organization's strategy particulars:

- Applying the assessment of choice, and creating a representation of the current and desired target states for the strategy. Current and target states will include initiatives and their projected risk mitigation. A sample risk assessment (presented in detail in Chapter 5 – Cyber Risks and Controls) will be provided, but the indices of choice and risk quantification techniques will have to be provided by the Steering Committee.
- Creation of the strategy timeline, Gantt chart, and swimlane to be created by the Steering Committee. These will contain the strategic initiatives listed, broken down by strategic objective. The timeline will indicate milestones and timeframes associated with their projected completion. The swimlane will show the flow of the strategy creation as it moves through the various groups in the organization. Samples of a strategy timeline, Gantt chart, and swimlane are presented in Chapter 3 – Strategy Project Management, and will be included again here.
- A strategic plan progress reporting template, as shown in Chapter 2 – The 6 STEPs in Developing and Maintaining a Cybersecurity and a Cyber Resiliency Strategy to be developed by the Steering Committee. This will

FIGURE 8.1   The Six Development and Maintenance STEPs for a Cybersecurity and Cyber Resiliency Strategy.

> be created either on a quarterly basis or another reporting timeline that suits the organization. It will contain the mission/vision, the strategy principles, the strategic objectives decided upon, and a bulleted list of the major initiatives that comprise each objective.

A sample completed template RACI of all the tasks per STEP and a list of all the Steering Group members was provided in Chapter 3 – Strategy Project Management. Furthermore, the specific responsibilities of each of the Steering Committee members were assigned in the full RACI spreadsheet. This was only an example. It will be up to the Steering Committee to develop the following for their specific organizations:

- Required participating members of the Steering Committee
- List of tasks broken down by specific STEP for all 6 STEPs
- The RACI assignments per Steering Committee member for each of the tasks in all 6 STEPs

In Chapter 1 – Why Cybersecurity and Cyber Resiliency Strategies are Mandatory for Organizations Today, a sample Enterprise Security Architecture was presented. It's critical for the Steering Committee to understand the information security architecture of the organization and its technical architecture composition together with its array of security products. As explained, this will enable them to see where there are architectural deficiencies that would inhibit the desired level of cyberattack mitigation. It would also show where there may be excessive resources deployed, rendering potentially an unbalanced resiliency effort. A current and target state architecture should be developed as a project by perhaps an architecture and/or engineering group to illustrate the progress of the strategy on the overall security posture.

In Chapter 1 – Why Cybersecurity and Cyber Resiliency Strategies are Mandatory for Organizations Today, a sample Regulatory Architecture was presented. The Steering Committee will need to determine which financial, legal, security, privacy, audit, Federal, Securities and Exchange Commission (SEC), etc., regulations would apply to the organizations' cybersecurity and cyber resiliency strategy. Today's Chief Information Officers (CIOs), Chief Executive Officers (CEOs), Chief Operating Officers (COOs), and Chief Technology Officers (CTOs) can be legally liable for not adhering to certain regulations. In some cases, noncompliance can result in fines or penalties as a result of certain regulations.

Now each of the 6 STEPs will be broken down into individual tasks to aide in the creation of the final Strategy document deliverable and drive the analysis.

8.2 STEP 1: PREPLANNING: PREPARATION FOR STRATEGY DEVELOPMENT

8.2.1 PREPLANNING CHECKLIST

Table 8.1 lists the major steps and decisions that the Steering Group may have to make to initiate the creation of the cybersecurity and cyber resiliency strategies. This checklist will need to be discussed and adjusted to fit your organization.

TABLE 8.1
Strategy Preplanning Checklist

- ☑ Form a Steering Committee – Designate the key players from top management (see Table 2.1 Steering Committee Members).
- ☑ Designate the Project Manager for the Steering Committee.
- ☑ Identify the appropriate SMEs to be included in the Steering Committee.
- ☑ Agree on corporate culture characteristics, analyze organizational type (Siloed, Matrixed, etc.) – become aware of organization's position on risk (see Figure 8.3).
- ☑ Review Figure 2.5 Organizational Readiness for Cyber Strategy to determine if all the STEPs for strategy development by the organization in general have been executed.
- ☑ Develop the strategy's critical success factors. These will be used later when evaluating Strategy Performance.
- ☑ Start to come to consensus in developing the Steering Committee Tasks. Use the 6 STEPs to organize the tasks.
- ☑ Present and discuss the corporate business values. Agree that the strategy must incorporate them. They also will be used to evaluate strategy performance.
- ☑ Determine the overall mission/vision of the strategy. Review Figure 8.2 as a guide.
- ☑ Identify the applicable cybersecurity, cyber resiliency, and architectural principles that apply to the strategy.
- ☑ Gain an understanding of the Security and Resiliency architectures so that they can be considered when creating the security objectives and initiatives.
- ☑ Understand all the legal and regulatory guidelines that may apply to the creation and implementation of the strategies.
- ☑ Derived from the Principles, develop the specific strategic objectives that will achieve the mission of the strategy. Break them down by cybersecurity objectives and cyber resiliency objectives.
- ☑ For each strategic objective, start to identify the individual initiatives and projects that will achieve each of them. Some will already be in progress.
- ☑ Perform an enterprise inventory of all cybersecurity and cyber resiliency strategies being planned, in the works, and already published.
- ☑ Ensure that there is representation of each major effort within the Steering Committee roster.
- ☑ Develop an alignment matrix that indicates areas of agreement and areas of divergence. This can be included as an Appendix in the final Strategy deliverable.

FIGURE 8.2   Mission/Vision, Principles, Strategic Objectives, and Initiatives Pyramid.

8.2.2   MISSION/VISION, PRINCIPLES, STRATEGIC OBJECTIVES, AND INITIATIVES PYRAMID

Use Figure 8.2 to set the structure of the strategy. A structure with more layers can be used. The Steering Committee will decide on this.

8.2.3   ANALYZE ORGANIZATIONAL AND CULTURAL STRUCTURE

Using Figure 8.3, analyze your organization's corporate culture. This will set the tone for many decisions going forward. Determine if your organization has silos

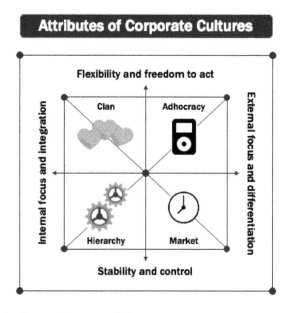

FIGURE 8.3   Attributes of Corporate Cultures.

and/or is matrixed, if the culture is pro or adverse risk. This may aid in determining who in senior management will need to be contacted and/or included in the strategy development in order to get eventual senior management buy-in.

8.2.4 RACI Completion for STEP 1

Break down the tasks for STEP 1: Preplanning- Preparation for Strategy Development as shown in Figure 8.4. This list of tasks will need to be adjusted to fit your Steering Committee's determination of the tasks for STEP 1. Then fill in the members of the Steering Committee. Complete the blank RACI diagram for STEP 1 in terms of tasks, Steering Committee Roles, and RACI responsibilities. Remember that RACIs can have only one Accountable (A) per task but each task can have multiple roles Responsible (R) for that task.

8.2.5 Critical Success Factors Validation

Table 8.2 is provided to help the Steering Committee examine each of the critical success factors derived in STEP 2 and demonstrate/document how the strategy contributes (or not) to each of the points. The factors are listed to provide a starting point for the Steering Committee to create their own critical success factors. This validation will be useful in measuring overall plan performance.

8.2.6 Evaluate Organizational Readiness

Evaluate organizational readiness according to Figure 8.5. Identify which items have been already addressed, which ones are in progress and which ones have not been considered yet. For those items that may not been addressed this year, they can become new initiatives under the Year 2 strategy umbrella.

8.3 STEP 2: STRATEGY PROJECT MANAGEMENT

8.3.1 Project Charter

Complete the blanked-out Project Charter in Figure 8.6 or create a more tailored one according to your organizations Project Management Office (PMO) procedures.

8.3.2 RACI Completion for STEP 2

Now complete the blank RACI for STEP 2 – Strategy Project Management, shown in Figure 8.7. Tasks are provided here, but this exercise requires that your organization's specific tasks, Steering Committee members, and their specific responsibilities be entered.

RACI - CYBERSECURITY AND CYBER RESILIENCY STRATEGY DEVELOPMENT AND MAINTENANCE

STEERING COMMITTEE ROLES

STEPS & TASKS	CISO	CIO	CRO	DR/BC	Bus. Resiliency	IT Infra	IT Tech	Biz P	PMO	Audit	Legal	Compliance	Risk
1 Formalize the Steering Committee members and Project Manager													
2 Agree on the Strategy Elements: the Pyramid													
3 Create the Mission/Vision Statement													
4 Create the Critical Success factors													
5 Determine the applicable corporate Business Values													
6 Agree on Corporate Culture positioning													
7 Identify the applicable Cybersecurity and Cyber Resiliency Principles													
8 Create the Cybersecurity and Cyber Resiliency Strategic Objectives													
9 Create the Cybersecurity and Cyber Resiliency strategic initiatives													
10 Document the Steering Committee Reponsibilities													

STEP 1 - PREPLANNING - PREPARATION FOR STRATEGY DEVELOPMENT

FIGURE 8.4   Blank RACI for STEP 1: Preplanning – Preparation for Strategy Development.

TABLE 8.2
Sample Critical Success Factors Validation

- Reduce residual risk
- Completed by due date
- Meets stated objectives or requirements
- Compliant with relevant regulations, standards, and policies
- Reduce resource opportunity cost
- Aligns with approved cyber strategies
- Maintain budgetary constraints
- Supported by senior management
- Efficient use of resources
- Approved by all parties
- Maps to corporate goals

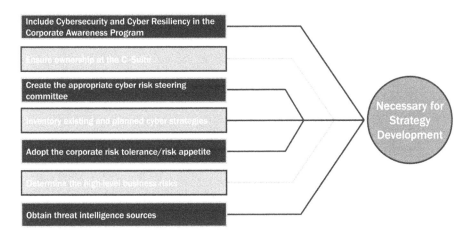

FIGURE 8.5 Organizational Readiness for a Cyber Strategy.

Project Charter					
Project Name	Cybersecurity and Cyber Resiliency Strategy			Project Manager	
Start Date		End Date		Project Sponsor	
Business Need					
Scope			Deliverables		
Potential Risks			Assumptions		
Schedule					
Budget or Resource Commitments					

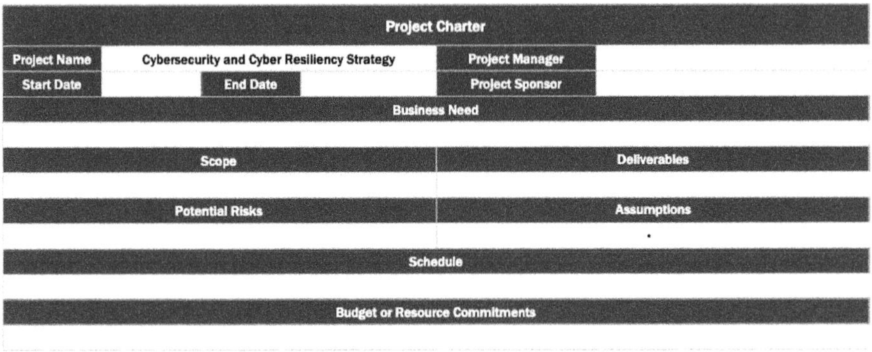

FIGURE 8.6 Blank STEP 2: Project Charter.

RACI - CYBERSECURITY AND CYBER RESILIENCY STRATEGY DEVELOPMENT AND MAINTENANCE

STEERING COMMITTEE ROLES

STEPS & TASKS

		CISO	CIO	CRO	Dev/SC	Business Operations	IT Infrastructure	Telecom	Procurement	HRO	Audit	Legal	Compliance	SMO
STEP 2 - STRATEGY PROJECT MANAGEMENT	11	Create the Strategy Project Charter												
	12	Identify existing and planned cybersecurity and cyber resiliency strategies												
	13	Prepare an Alignment Matrix												
	14	Develop a Strategy Timeline and Gantt Chart												
	15	Develop a Strategy Swimlane												
	16	Create the Operational RACI for all the Steering Committee tasks												
	17	Map the Initiatives to the NIST CSF												
	18	Create outline of Final Strategy Deliverable												

FIGURE 8.7   Blank RACI for STEP 2: Strategy Project Management.

8.3.3 COMPLETE RACI DEVELOPMENT FOR THE STEERING COMMITTEE TASKS

The completed RACI in Chapter 2 is an example and will need to be modified and filled in by the Steering Committee or their designees. The personnel composition of the members of the Steering Committee may be different than the one presented in Chapter 3, and the tasks that the Steering Committee derives may also be different – therefore the RACI provided may not be exactly representative of the organization. By filling in an accurate and organizationally appropriate RACI, all will better understand the tasks required and who is responsible for each of them. The objective of this exercise is to fill in and fine tune all the Steering Committee participants, all the tasks that need to be done per STEP, and to assign the individual responsibilities. Figure 8.8a–e is presented here in its complete form as an example. The values may not be correct for your organization.

8.3.4 DATA FLOW ANALYSIS FOR STEP 2

The diagram for STEP 2 Data Flow Analysis was presented in Chapter 3. It is shown again as Figure 8.9. Now modify it to fit your organization.

8.3.5 DEVELOP DRAFT FINAL DELIVERABLE TABLE OF CONTENTS

Use Table 8.3 as a starting point.

8.4 STEPs 3 AND 4: CYBER THREATS, VULNERABILITIES, INTELLIGENCE ANALYSIS, RISKS, AND CONTROLS

8.4.1 RACI FOR STEPs 3 AND 4: CYBER THREATS, VULNERABILITIES & CYBER RISKS, AND CONTROLS

Complete the blank RACI for STEP 3 and STEP 4 in Figures 8.10 and 8.11 respectively.

8.4.2 DATA FLOW ANALYSIS FOR STEPs 3 AND 4

Figure 8.12 was presented in Chapter 3. Now modify it to represent your organization.

8.4.3 INCIDENTS TO CONTROLS MAPPING

STEPs 3 and 4 examined the intertwining of threats, vulnerabilities, risks, and controls. Controls were further broken down into deterrent, preventative, detective, corrective, predictive, and containment controls.

RACI – CYBERSECURITY AND CYBER RESILIENCY STRATEGY DEVELOPMENT AND MAINTENANCE

STEPS & TASKS		CISO	CIO	CFO	ORM/RE	Tech Resiliency	IT Mktg	IT Arch	Arch	PMO	Arch	Legal	Outsourcer	SME
						STEERING COMMITTEE ROLES								
1	Formalize the Steering Committee members and Project Manager	A,R	R	R	C	C	C	C	I	C	I	I	I	I
2	Agree on the strategy elements: the Pyramid	A,R	R	R	C	C	C	C	I	I	I	I	I	I
3	Create the mission/vision statement	A,R	R	R	C	C	C	C	I	I	I	I	I	I
4	Create the critical success factors	A,R	R	R	C	C	C	C	I	I	I	I	I	I
5	Determine the applicable corporate business values	R	A,R	R	C	C	C	C	I	I	I	I	I	I
6	Agree on corporate culture positioning	A	R	R	I	C	C	C	I	I	C	C	C	I
7	Identify the applicable cybersecurity and cyber resiliency principles	A	R	R	R	R	C	C	C	I	C	C	C	I
8	Create the cybersecurity and cyber resiliency strategic objectives	A	R	R	R	R	C	C	I	I	C	C	C	I
9	Create the cybersecurity and cyber resiliency initiatives	R	A,R	C	R	R	R	R	I	I	C	I	I	C
10	Document the Steering Committee responsibilities	R	A,R	R	R	C	C	C	I	R	C	C	C	I

STEP 1 – PREPLANNING – PREPARATION FOR STRATEGY DEVELOPMENT

(Continued)

FIGURE 8.8   Sample RACI Diagram: a) STEP 1.

FIGURE 8.8 (Continued) Sample RACI Diagram: b) STEP 2.

RACI - CYBERSECURITY AND CYBER RESILIENCY STRATEGY DEVELOPMENT AND MAINTENANCE

STEERING COMMITTEE ROLES

STEP 2 - STRATEGY PROJECT MANAGEMENT

#	STEPS & TASKS	CISO	CIO									Complexity
11	Create the Strategy Project Charter	A,R	R	C	C	C	C	R	I	I		I
12	Identify existing and planned cybersecurity and cyber resiliency strategies	A	R	C	C	C	I	I	I	I		C
13	Prepare an alignment matrix	A	R	C	R	C	I	I	I	I		C
14	Develop a strategy timeline and Gantt chart	A	C	C	C	C	C	R	I	I		I
15	Develop a strategy swimlane	A,R	C	C	C	C	C	R	C	C	C	I
16	Create the operational RACI for all the Steering Committee tasks	A,R	C	C	C	C	C	R	C	C	C	I
17	Map the initiatives to the NIST CSF	A,R	R	R	R	C	C	R	C	C	C	I
18	Create outline of final strategy deliverable	A,R	R	R	C	C	C	R	C	C	C	I

(Continued)

RACI - CYBERSECURITY AND CYBER RESILIENCY STRATEGY DEVELOPMENT AND MAINTENANCE

STEPS & TASKS		CISO	CTO	CRO	DR&BC	Bus. Resiliency	IT Infra.	IT Arch.	Prod.	R&D	Audit	Legal	Compliance	SME
						STEERING COMMITTEE ROLES								
STEP 3 - CYBER THREATS, VULNERABILITIES & INTELLIGENCE ANALYSIS	19	Determine the current business threats in priority order	A,R	R	R	R	R	R	R	C	I	C	C	C	C
	20	Determine the current business vulnerabilities in priority order	A,R	R	R	R	R	R	R	C	I	C	C	C	C
	21	Analyze the process for current threat intelligence	R	A,R	R	C	R	R	R	C	I	C	C	C	C
STEP 4 - CYBER RISKS & CONTROLS	22	Acknowledge enterprise risk tolerance and risk appetite standards and apply to the strategy	R	R	A,R	C	C	C	C	I	I	I	I	I	C
	23	Agree on a risk measurement methodology or accept the corporate standard	R	R	A,R	C	C	C	C	I	I	C	I	I	C
	24	Create the Cyber Key Risk Indicators (KRI) and Key Performance Indicators (KPI)	R	R	A,R	C	C	C	C	I	I	C	I	I	C
	25	Take an inventory on how controls are implemented and monitored	R	R	R	C	C	A	C	I	I	R	C	R	C
	26	Correlate risks, threats and vulnerabilities to controls	R	R	A,R	C	R	C	C	I	I	R	I	C	C

(Continued)

FIGURE 8.8 (Continued)   Sample RACI Diagram: c) STEPs 3 and 4.

RACI - CYBERSECURITY AND CYBER RESILIENCY STRATEGY DEVELOPMENT AND MAINTENANCE

STEERING COMMITTEE ROLES

STEPS & TASKS											
STEP 5 - ASSESSING THE CURRENT & TARGET STATES											
27	Inventory all cyber related assessments past, present and future	R	R	C	R	C	C	C	A	C	C	I
28	Evaluate and decide on assessment types to be used in determining current & target states	A,R	C	R	C	C	C	I	I	I	I	C
29	Decide on which assessment types will be recognized/adopted	R	A,R	R	C	C	C	I	I	C	C	C
30	Create assessment schedules to determine future plan performance	R	A,R	R	C	C	C	I	I	C	C	C
31	Agree on the high level cyber program	R	A,R	R	R	R	C	I	I	I	I	C
32	Agree on the adoption of NIST CSF for the main cyber framework	A,R	C	C	I	C	C	R	R	I	C	C
33	Assess current and target states	A,R	R	R	R	R	C	I	I	C	C	R

FIGURE 8.8 (Continued)   Sample RACI Diagram: d) STEP 5.

(Continued)

RACI - CYBERSECURITY AND CYBER RESILIENCY STRATEGY DEVELOPMENT AND MAINTENANCE

STEERING COMMITTEE ROLES

STEPS & TASKS		CISO	CTO	CRO	DPO/DPC	Bus. Leaders	IT Infra	IT Arch	PMO	Audit	Legal	Compliance	SMEs
34	Complete the yearly strategy progress report	A,R	R	R	C	C	I	I	I	R	I	C	C
35	Ensure compliance with regulations	A	R	R	R	R	R	R	R	C	C	C	I
36	Prepare the EoY Strategy Performance Measurement Plan (KRIs, KPIs) and Critical Success Factors metrics	A,R	R	R	C	C	C	C	R	C	C	C	R
37	Determine corporate governance requirements	A,R	R	R	I	I	I	I	R	C	C	C	I
38	Schedule reviews with governance bodies	R	R	R	I	I	I	I	A	C	C	C	I
39	Distribute EoY reports to senior management	A,R	I	I	I	I	I	I	R	I	I	I	I
40	Create additional strategy performance reports	A,R	C	C	C	C	C	I	I	C	I	I	C
41	Establish objectives for the following year	A,R	R	R	C	C	C	I	R	C	I	I	C
42	Create list of possible new initiatives for following year	A,R	R	R	R	R	R	C	R	I	I	R	R
43	Confirm Steering Group Committee member composition going forward	A,R	C	C	C	C	C	C	I	C	C	C	I
44	Create timeline for following year	A	R	C	I	I	I	I	R	I	I	C	I

STEP 6 - MEASURING STRATEGIC PLAN PERFORMANCE & EOY TASKS

FIGURE 8.8 (Continued)   Sample RACI Diagram: e) STEP 6.

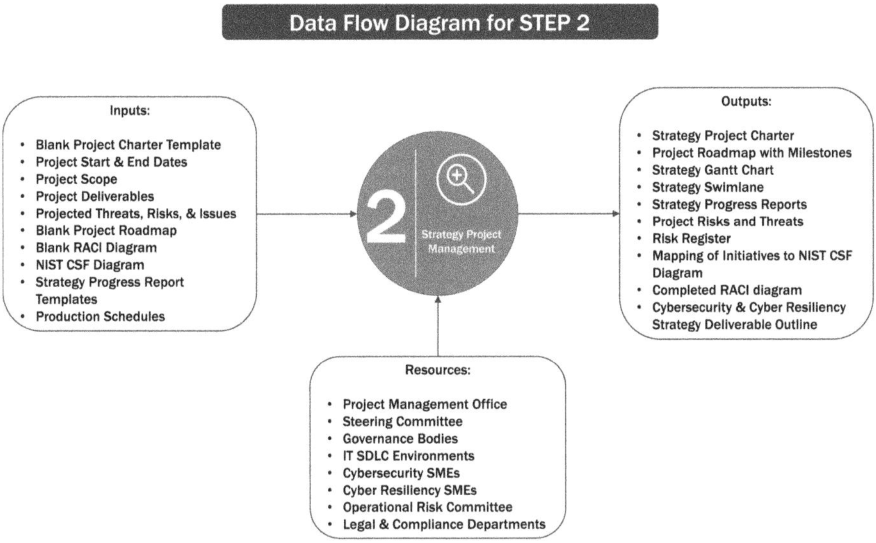

FIGURE 8.9   Sample Data Flow Diagram for STEP 2.

Figure 8.13 is presented to show that controls can be directed at specific types of incidents (threat, vulnerability, risk, or issue), and in some cases, there exists a one-to-many relationship.

Create a similar mapping of controls to incident types, but break down further the threats, vulnerabilities, and risks/issues of your organization into subcategories. In this way, it can be seen if there exist specific and adequate controls per incident sub-type.

8.5   STEP 5: CURRENT AND TARGET STATE ASSESSMENTS

8.5.1   RACI FOR STEP 5: CURRENT AND TARGET STATE ASSESSMENTS

Fill in Figure 8.14. Be sure to adjust the tasks for your organization.

8.5.2   DATA FLOW ANALYSIS FOR STEP 5: CURRENT AND TARGET STATE ASSESSMENTS

Fill in Figure 8.15.

8.5.3   PERFORMING A QUANTITATIVE RISK ASSESSMENT

Chapter 5 – Cyber Risks and Controls gave an example of a how to perform a risk assessment of an organization's assets. Figure 8.16 is a partially filled-in assessment spreadsheet.

TABLE 8.3

Sample Cybersecurity and Cyber Resiliency Strategy TOC Final Deliverable Outline

1. Executive Summary
2. Introduction
3. Cybersecurity and Cyber Resiliency Definitions
4. Components of Cybersecurity and Cyber Resiliency
5. Current Information Security Architecture and Cyber Regulatory Architecture
6. Cyber IT areas requiring preplanning
7. Steering Group Committee
   a. Members and Responsibilities
   b. Committee Charter
   c. RACI Strategy Development Template Chart
   d. Corporate Culture and Values discussion
   e. Critical Success Factors determination
8. Purpose and Objectives of the Cybersecurity and Cyber Resiliency Strategies
   a. Mission/Vision, Principles, Strategic Objectives, and Initiatives Pyramid
      i. Mission/Vision
      ii. Principles
      iii. Strategic Objectives
      iv. Initiatives/Projects
   b. National Institute of Standards and Technology (NIST) Cybersecurity Framework (CSF) Mapping of Initiatives to Capabilities to Strategic Objectives
9. Methodology for Strategy Development with Definitions
   a. The 6 STEPs for Cybersecurity and Cyber Resiliency Strategy Development
      i. STEP 1: Preplanning – Preparation for Strategy Development
      ii. STEP 2: Strategy Project Management
      iii. STEP 3: Cyber Threats, Vulnerabilities, and Intelligence Analysis
      iv. STEP 4: Cyber Risks and Controls
      v. STEP 5: Assessing Current and Target States
      vi. STEP 6: Measuring Strategic Plan Performance and EoY Tasks
10. Strategy Project Management
    a. Alignment evaluation with other existing corporate cyber strategies
    b. High-Level Timeline with Milestones
    c. Strategy Development Timeline showing Progress
    d. Draft Gantt Chart
    e. Strategy Development Project Swimlane
    f. Full Project RACI with Steering Committee and tasks by STEPs
11. Cyber Threats and Vulnerabilities Analysis
    a. Analysis of Current Cyber Threats
    b. Analysis of Current Vulnerabilities
    c. Analysis of Cyber Attacks
12. Cyber Risk Analysis
    a. Analysis of Cyber Risks
    b. Corporate Risk Appetite and Risk Tolerance
    c. Corporate Cyber Risk Measurement Methodologies
    d. NIST 800-30 Cyber Risk Measurement Example

(Continued)

TABLE 8.3 *(Continued)*

Sample Cybersecurity and Cyber Resiliency Strategy TOC Final Deliverable Outline

13. Cyber Controls Analysis
    a. Analysis of Cyber Controls
    b. Mapping of Threats/Vulnerabilities to Risks and Controls
    c. Cyber Insurance Policy
14. Assessing NIST CSF Current and Target States
    a. Standards and Frameworks Used
    b. Methodologies and Metrics
    c. NIST CSF Assessment Measuring Current and Target State
    d. Discussion of Mapped and Un-Mapped Initiatives
    e. Maturity Rating Quantitative Methods
15. Measuring Plan Performance
    a. Comparisons against:
        i. Business Objectives
        ii. Critical Success Factors
        iii. Strategy Alignment
        iv. Project Progress against Strategic Objectives
        v. Audit/Security Issues and Findings
        vi. Findings Closed
        vii. Increase in Risk Mitigation per assets and initiatives
        viii. Cyber Key Risk Indicators (KRIs)
        ix. Cyber Key Performance Indicators (KPIs)
        x. NIST 800-30 Cyber Risk Measurement Methodology Evaluations
16. Project Reporting
    a. Sample Strategy Progress Report
    b. Yearly Strategy Performance Report
    c. Strategic Objective Completion
    d. Business Unit Quarterly Risk Mitigation
    e. Cybersecurity and Cyber Resiliency Initiative Progress
17. End of Year (EoY) Tasks
    a. Complete RACI for upcoming year
    b. Define the Strategy's Pyramid Parameters for Following Year
    c. Create the Timeline for the Following year
    d. Confirm Steering Group Member Composition
    e. Ensure Compliance with relevant Regulations
18. New Initiatives
    a. Methodology
    b. Suggested Cybersecurity and Cyber Resiliency New Initiatives & Reasoning
19. Governance Review
    a. Determine Governance Review Bodies and their reporting relationships
    b. Timeline for Governance Review
    c. Governance Bodies Roles and Responsibilities RACI
    d. Swimlane for Governance Review by Governance Body
20. Appendices
    a. Enterprise Strategy Alignment Matrix
    b. Full RACI for Complete Project

RACI - CYBERSECURITY AND CYBER RESILIENCY STRATEGY DEVELOPMENT AND MAINTENANCE

STEPS & TASKS		STEERING COMMITTEE ROLES												
		CISO	CTO	CRO	DR/BC	Bus. Resilience	IT Infra.	IT Arch.	Prod.	PMO	Audit.	Legal	Controllers	SME
STEP 3 : CYBER THREATS, VULNERABILITIES & INTELLIGENCE ANALYSIS	19	Determine the current business threats in priority order												
	20	Determine the current business vulnerabilities in priority ordrer												
	21	Analyze the process for current Threat Intelligence												

FIGURE 8.10 Blank RACI for STEP 3: Cyber Threats, Vulnerabilities, and Intelligence Analysis.

RACI - CYBERSECURITY AND CYBER RESILIENCY STRATEGY DEVELOPMENT AND MAINTENANCE

STEERING COMMITTEE ROLES

STEPS & TASKS										
STEP 4 - CYBER RISKS & CONTROLS	22	Acknowledge enterprise risk tolerance and risk appetite standards and apply to strategy								
	23	Agree on a risk measurement methodology or accept the corporate standard								
	24	Create the Cyber Key Risk Indicators (KRI) and Key Performance Indicators (KPI)								
	25	Take an inventory on how Controls are implemented and monitored								
	26	Correlate Risks, Threats and Vulnerabilities to Controls								

FIGURE 8.11 Blank RACI for STEP 4: Cyber Risks and Controls.

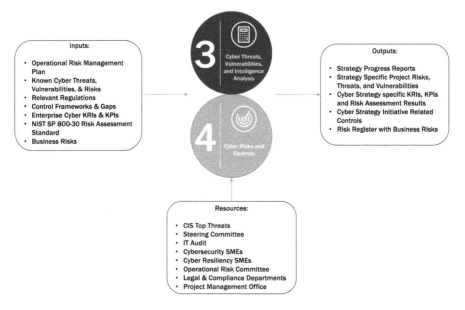

FIGURE 8.12   Sample Data Flow Diagram for STEPs 3 and 4.

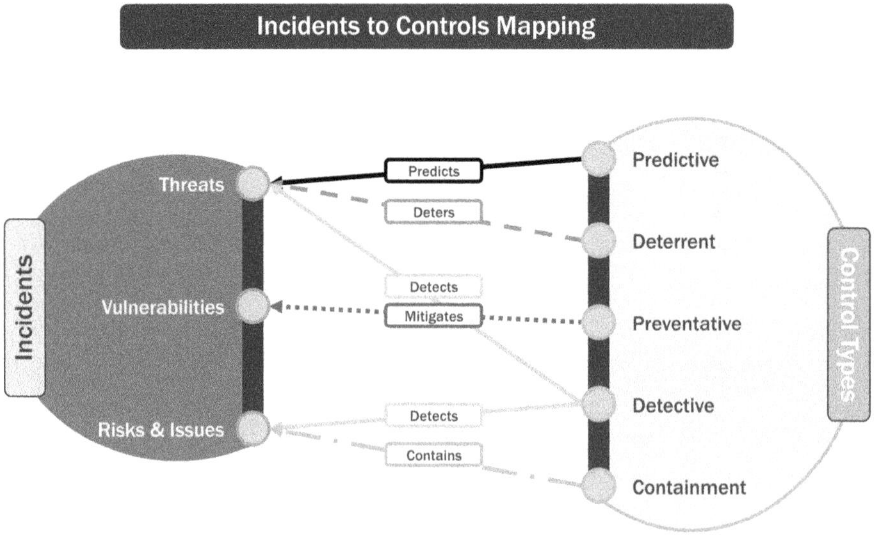

Incidents to Controls Mapping

FIGURE 8.13   Incidents to Controls Mapping.

RACI - CYBERSECURITY AND CYBER RESILIENCY STRATEGY DEVELOPMENT AND MAINTENANCE															
STEPS & TASKS			STEERING COMMITTEE ROLES												
			CISO	CTO	CRO	DR/BC	Bus. Resiliency	IT Infra.	IT Arch.	Prod.	PMO	Audit	Legal	Compliance	SME
STEP 5 - ASSESSING THE CURRENT & TARGET STATES	27	Inventory all cyber related assessments past, present and future													
	28	Evaluate and decide on assessment types to be used in determining Current & Target states													
	29	Conduct a current state assessment using the NIST Computer Security Framework (CSF) mapping current initiatives to Capabilities													
	30	Analyze the NIST CSF Mappings and discuss results: mapped and unmapped initiatives and their implications													
	31	Diagram the Current and desired Target NIST CSF Tier Ratings (1-4)													
	32	Create assessment schedules to determine future plan perfomance													
	33	Assess Current, Target and EoY States													

FIGURE 8.14 Blank RACI for STEP 5: Assessing Current and Target States.

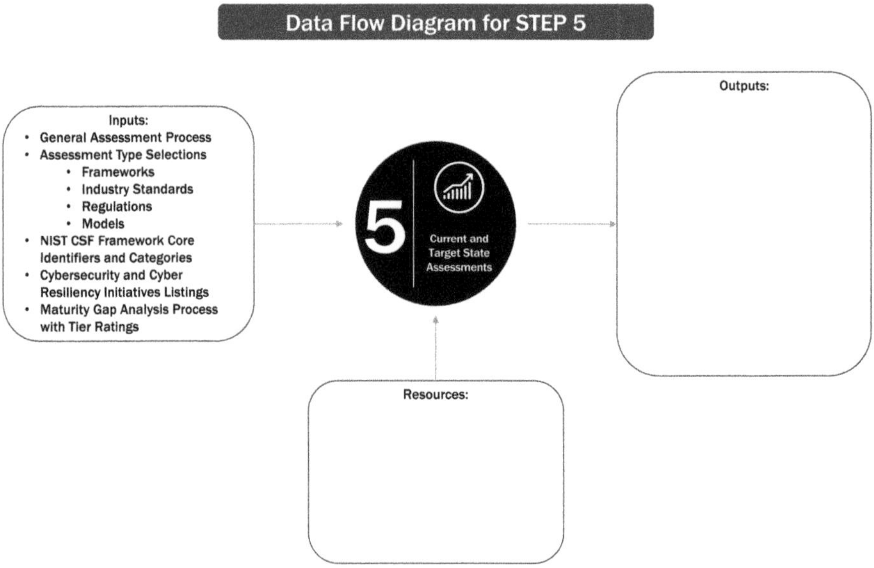

FIGURE 8.15   Partial Data Flow Diagram for STEP 5: Assessing Current and Target States.

Follow the directions below and create your own assessment:

1. *ASSETS*
    a. Identify the assets of importance (high value)
    b. Identify some assets of lesser value in order to see the difference in the final Risk Rating result
    c. List assets in Column B
    d. Rate the asset values
2. *THREATS*
    a. Identify a number of top threats facing the organization
    b. List the Threats across Row 7 in columns
    c. Review the Center for Internet Security (CIS) Top 20 Threats as examples
    d. Set the Rating Scales for the threats
        i. Threat Rating (1–10)
        ii. Probability of occurrence of each threat (x%)
        iii. Impact magnitude of each threat (1–5)
    e. Rate each threat (1–10)
    f. Assign a % of probability of occurrence to each threat
    g. Assign an impact magnitude for each threat
3. *THREAT CALCULATIONS*
    a. For each threat, multiply: The Threat Rating × Probability of Occurrence × Impact Magnitude × Asset Value

CUSTOMIZED NIST 800-30 CYBER RISK ASSESSMENT EXAMPLE

		THREATS				VULNERABILITIES Vulnerability Severity (1 = Low, 5 = Critical)					TOTAL RISK SCORE (Sum of Cell Values for Assets)	RISK RATING RESULT
		Unauthorized Use / Access - Account Compromised	Misuse of information by Authorized Users	Data leaks/ PII Exposure	Loss of Data	Service/ Productivity Disruptions	Sensitive Data Exposure	Data Theft	Injection	Failure to System Patch	Security Mis-Configuration		High, Medium, Low
Threat Rating (1- Low, 10 = High)		4	5	8	9	10						L = 110 or less M = 111-190 H = over 190	
Probability of Occurance (%)		25%	25%	50%	15%	2%							
Impact Magnitude (1 = Negligable, 5 = High)		5	4	5	3	5	5	4	3	3	3		
ASSETS: People, Processes, Technology	Asset Value (1-5)												
Human Resources Data - People and Organization	3												
Network Infrastructure	4.5												
Project Management Processes	2.5												
Financial - Data Repositories	4.5												
E-Commerce - Information Systems	2.5												
System Life Cycle Environments	3.5												
Cyber Policies, Standards and Procedures	3												
Financial Applications	4.5												
External/InternetCommunications Links	4.5												
Data Center IT Infrastructure	4.5												
BU Self-Assessment Processes	2.5												
Cybersecurity Software	5												

FIGURE 8.16 Partial Cyber Risk Assessment Example.

    b.   This result is value of the threat for this asset. In the case of the first asset – Human Resources, calculate the formula

    c.   The value 15 goes in the first column under the Unauthorized Use threat and to the right of the first asset – Human Resources

    d.   Continue across the spreadsheet for each threat for Human Resources

    e.   Then proceed down the list of assets and perform the same multiplication filling in all the boxes under Threats

4. *VULNERABILITIES*

    a.   In the Vulnerabilities section of the spreadsheet, list the most important Vulnerability types and their corresponding severity rating (1–5)

    b.   The values opposite each asset in the vulnerabilities section then become:

        i.   The Asset value × the Vulnerability type's rating

       ii.   Calculate the value for Human Resources

    c.   Fill in the remainder of the Vulnerability ratings for each asset

5. *TOTAL RISK SCORE*

    a.   To arrive at the Total Risk Score per asset, sum the numbers across the spreadsheet for each asset (include the numbers for both the threats and the vulnerabilities). Calculate the sum for Human Resources

6. *RISK RATING RESULT*

    a.   Derive a scale from the resultant numbers, differentiating them into buckets of High, Medium, and Low (HML) (or any other type of rating desired). See Table 8.4.

    b.   Classify all the assets High, Medium, or Low according to their scores

    c.   All assets have now been risk assessed using this methodology and can be addressed accordingly in terms of controls

---

TABLE 8.4
NIST Adversarial Threat Ratings

Qualitative Values	Description
Very High	The adversary has a very sophisticated level of expertise, is well resourced, and can generate opportunities to support multiple successful, continuous, and coordinated attacks.
High	The adversary has a sophisticated level of expertise, with significant resources and opportunities to support multiple successful coordinated attacks.
Moderate	The adversary has moderate resources, expertise, and opportunities to support multiple successful attacks.
Low	The adversary has limited resources, expertise, and opportunities to support a successful attack.
Very Low	The adversary has very limited resources, expertise, and opportunities to support a successful attack.

8.6   STEP 6: MEASURING PLAN PERFORMANCE AND EoY TASKS

8.6.1   Checklist for STEP 6: End of Year Tasks

Use the checklist in Table 8.5 to help manage the preplanning phases during the EoY tasks.

8.6.2   RACI for STEP 6: Measuring Plan Performance and EoY Tasks

Fill in the blank RACI for STEP 6: Measuring Plan Performance and EoY Tasks shown in Figure 8.17. Adjust the tasks to suit your needs and goals.

8.6.3   Data Flow Diagram for STEP 6: Measuring Strategic Plan Performance and EoY Tasks

Finish Figure 8.18.

8.6.4   Derive the Critical Success Factors

Use the critical success factors previously identified and shown again in Table 8.6 as an example and see how many and to what degree they have been achieved. Adjust

---

TABLE 8.5
Checklist for EoY Tasks

☑ Ensure compliance with regulations
☑ Complete Governance hoops
  • Identify Governance Bodies
  • Understand lead times necessary for Governance Reviews
  • Schedule meetings with Governance Bodies
☑ Prepare the EoY Performance Measurement Plan Metrics
  • KPIs
  • KRIs
  • Critical Success Factors
  • Initiative Progress against Strategic Objectives correlated to the CSF
☑ Prepare EoY Status Reports
☑ Distribute EoY Plan Performance and the Yearly Strategy Overview Reports to Senior Management
☑ Prepare for Next Year
  • Confirm Steering Group member composition
  • Establish objectives for next year
  • Create list of possible new initiatives for following year
  • Create possible list of initiatives to retire or phase out as a result of the Yearly Performance results
  • Create timeline for following year
  • Be aware of any new Standards or Regulations that will be issued in the following years

---

			STEERING COMMITTEE ROLES														
STEPS & TASKS		CISO	CTO	CRO	LoR/BC	Bus-Resiliency	IT-Infra	IT-Arch	Proc	PMO	Audit	Legal	Compliance	SME
34	Complete the Yearly Strategy Overview Report													
35	Ensure Compliance with Regulations													
36	Prepare the EOY Strategy Performance Measurement Plan: KRIs, KPIs, and Critical Success Factors Metrics													
37	Determine corporate Governance requirements													
38	Schedule reviews with Governance bodies													
39	Distribute EOY Reports to Senior Management													
40	Create additional Strategy Performance reports													
41	Establish Objectives for the following year													
42	Create list of possible new initiatives for following year													
43	Confirm Steering Group Committee member composition going forward													
44	Create Timeline for following year													

RACI - CYBERSECURITY AND CYBER RESILIENCY STRATEGY DEVELOPMENT AND MAINTENANCE

STEP 6 - MEASURING STRATEGIC PLAN PERFORMANCE & EOY TASKS

FIGURE 8.17　Blank RACI for STEP 6: Measuring Strategic Plan Performance and EoY Tasks.

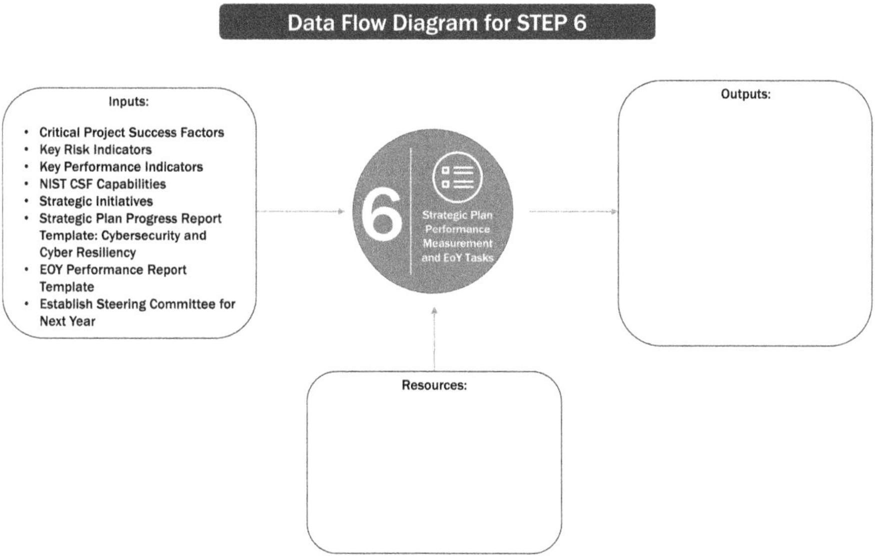

FIGURE 8.18 Partial Data Flow Diagram for STEP 6: Measuring Strategic Plan Performance and EoY tasks.

and/or weight them for your organization. Develop new ones for the subsequent year or carry these forward as desired.

8.6.5 Review the Key Risk Indicators and Key Performance Indicators

See if the list of KRI indicators shown in Table 8.7 still holds true. Then see if the list of KPI indicators shown in Table 8.8 still holds true. Verify if they are accurate, complete, and still timely. If not, discuss with the appropriate parties how and when to update them. Remember, the KRIs and the KPIs have been developed at the enterprise level.

8.6.6 Strategic Plan Reporting Template

Use the examples shown in Chapter 7 for the Quarterly Strategy Progress Reports. This is shown again in Figure 8.19.

TABLE 8.6
Critical Success Factors

- Reduce residual risk
- Completed by due date
- Meets stated objectives or requirements
- Compliant with relevant regulations, standards, and policies
- Reduce opportunity cost

- Maintain budgetary constraints
- Supported by senior management
- Efficient use of resources
- Approved by all parties
- Maps to corporate goals
- Aligns with approved Cyber strategies

TABLE 8.7
Sample Key Risk Indicators

Key Risk Indicator	Unit of Measurement	Progress
Incident Response	Mean time to detect and respond	% increase/decrease
Security Architecture	# of Business Units adopting a cyber resilient architecture	% increase/decrease
Key Controls Adoption	# of key security controls implemented yearly	% increase/decrease
Audit Findings	% increase/decrease in # of cyber-related audit findings	% findings closed out of total; % increase in findings
Threat Intelligence	Increase/decrease in quality and quantity of threat intelligence	# Alerts responded to in a timely basis as a % of the whole
Third Party Risk Management	# of business partners seen as generally effective	% increase/decrease
Security Awareness	% of employees completed cyber security training	% increase/decrease total # of employees
Regulations & Compliance	% of mandatory regulations complied with this year	% increase/decrease of total required regulations

TABLE 8.8
Sample Cyber Key Performance Indicators (KPI)

Key Performance Indicator	Unit of Measurement	Progress
Cybersecurity Strategy	% of Business Units adoption of the strategy out of total applicable Bus	% increase/decrease from last year
Cyber Resiliency Strategy	% of Business Units adoption of the strategy out of total applicable Bus	% increase/decrease from last year
Threat Exposure	Documenting high-risk categories % increase in high-risk categories/year	% high-risk categories addressed
Assessments and Penetration Tests	# of critical applications and systems tested and/or assessed as a % of total required	% increase/decrease
Audit Findings	% increase/decrease in # of cyber-related audit findings	% findings closed; % increase/decrease of new findings
Patch Management	# of security patches applied as % of total required	% increase/decrease in vulnerabilities
Privileged Accounts	# of privileged accounts removed	% increase/decrease in privileged accounts
Unauthorized Access	# of unauthorized access attempts	% increase/decrease of attempts

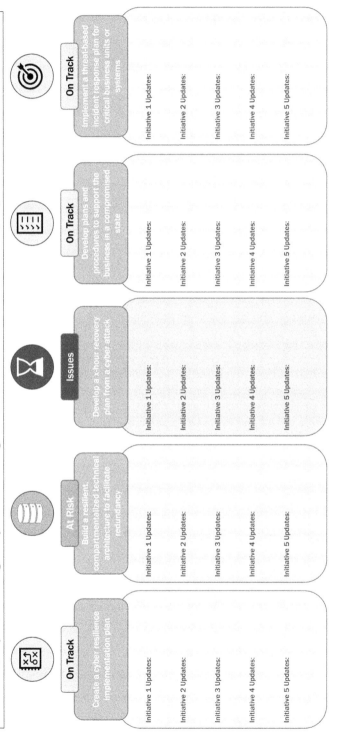

FIGURE 8.19 Strategy Progress Report – Cyber Resiliency.

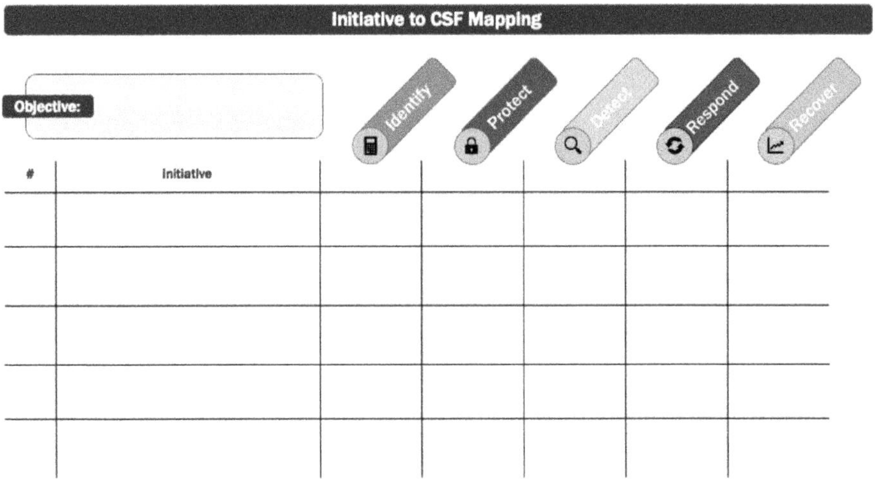

FIGURE 8.20   Blank Initiative to CSF Mapping per Objective.

8.6.7   INITIATIVE TO CSF MAPPING PER OBJECTIVE

As presented in Chapter 7, STEP 6, another view of performance reporting that can be presented to senior management is to provide a series of graphics which categorize the initiatives per CSF capability that comprise each strategic objective. In this fashion, one can see the CSF capability (Identify, Protect, Detect, Respond, and Recover) concentration of the strategic objective by showing each initiative and the corresponding capabilities in which the organization is investing.

Shown in Figure 8.20 is a blank template that can be used for each strategic objective.

8.6.8   CYBERSECURITY AND CYBER RESILIENCY YEARLY REPORT

Figure 8.21 shows a completed Cybersecurity and Cyber Resiliency Yearly Report. Calculate and alter the graphics to suit the current organizational numbers.

8.6.9   GOVERNANCE HOOPS

Getting Governance approval is always more complicated and time consuming than anticipated. Good project planning and reconnaissance will help greatly with this last step of the project.

8.6.10   GOVERNANCE APPROVAL ORGANIZATION HIERARCHY

Diagram the Governance Organization Hierarchy. Use Figure 8.22, originally presented in Chapter 7. Use it as a starting point to understand each area's roles, responsibilities and reporting structures.

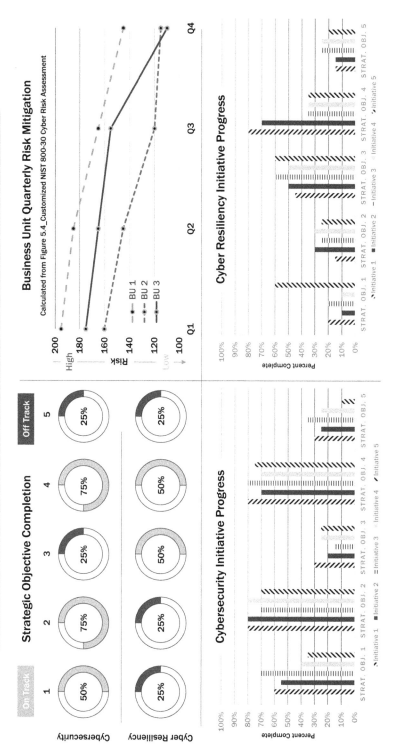

FIGURE 8.21 Cybersecurity and Cyber Resiliency Yearly Report.

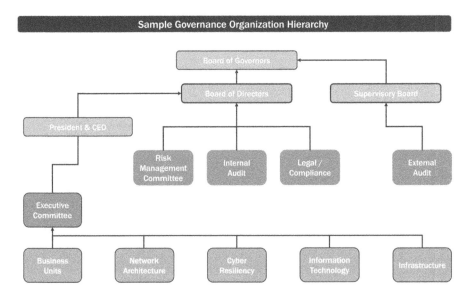

FIGURE 8.22   Sample Governance Organization Hierarchy.

8.6.11   GOVERNANCE APPROVAL RACI

Using the Governance RACI developed in Chapter 7, complete the Governance RACI shown in part in Figure 8.23. Ensure that the STEPs and tasks are those that your Governance Bodies perform.

8.6.12   GOVERNANCE APPROVAL SWIMLANE

After the Governance Organization Hierarchy chart is complete, a Governance Approval Swimlane must be created so that the approval order and path of the Cybersecurity and Cyber Resiliency Strategies can be understood and planned. The Swimlane will show all the approval steps required and in which order. Here the PMO comes into play in organizing the flow of the document and getting the document review on each agenda. Time also must be left for each feedback loop.

Complete Figure 8.24. This diagram was presented in its entirety in Chapter 7. Note that the Governance Approval Bodies are along the y-axis, but the flow through to the approval of the final Cybersecurity and Cyber Resiliency Strategy must be documented along the x-axis in a forward motion (left to right). The path must contain all decision-making checkpoints with feedback loops. Swimlane flowchart objects can represent groups, data, actions/procedures, decision points, and documents.

GOVERNANCE ROLES RACI

STEPS & TASKS	Business Units*	Steering Committee	Executive Committee	Risk Mgmt Committee	Internal Audit	Legal / Compliance	External Audit	President & CEO	Board of Directors	Supervisory Board	Board of Governors
Develop the Cybersecurity and Cyber Resilience Strategies											
Review/Comment on the Cybersecurity and Cyber Resilience Strategies											
Review/Comment and approve the Cybersecurity and Cyber Resilience Strategies											

* Business Units role assignments are equivalent to roles for Network Architecture, Cyber Resiliency, Information Technology, Infrastructure and any other business department contributing to the development of the Strategies under the Steering Committee

FIGURE 8.23 Blank Strategy Governance Approval RACI.

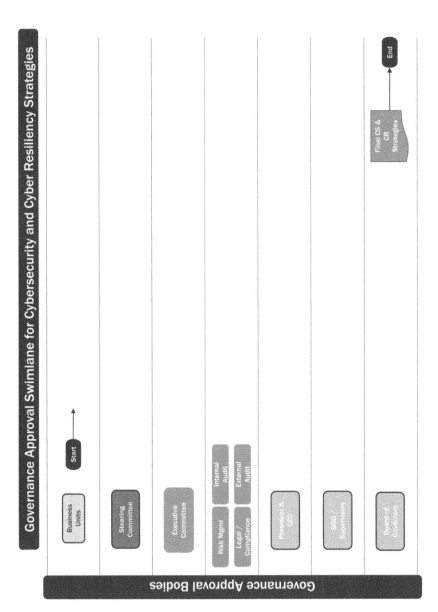

FIGURE 8.24   Blank Governance Approval Swimlane.

8.7   ASSEMBLING THE FULL PROJECT RACI

Assemble all the RACI Segments for the 6 STEPs. The end result should look similar to Figures 8.8a–e. Compare your organization's Roles, Steps, and Tasks to Figures 8.8a–e and add the Governance roles and responsibilities as well.

8.8   CHAPTER 8 DOWNLOADABLE FILES

Chapter 8 figures, templates, diagrams, etc., are saved in PDF format and are available for download from the CRC Press/Taylor and Francis, Inc. website after the purchase of the book: https://crcpress.com/9780367339456.

Milton Keynes UK
Ingram Content Group UK Ltd.
UKHW031531071024
449327UK00005B/130